CIVIL WAR
MARYLAND

CIVIL WAR
MARYLAND

STORIES FROM THE OLD LINE STATE

RICHARD P. COX

THE
History
PRESS

Published by The History Press
Charleston, SC 29403
www.historypress.net

Cover: Pratt Street Riot in Baltimore, April 19, 1861, from *Harper's Weekly*. *Courtesy of the Maryland State Archives*.

Cover design by Natasha Momberger.

All images courtesy of the author unless otherwise noted.

First published 2008
Second printing 2008
Third printing 2010
Fourth printing 2010
Fifth printing 2012

Manufactured in the United States

ISBN 978.1.59629.419.6

Library of Congress Cataloging-in-Publication Data

Cox, Richard P.
Civil War Maryland : stories from the Old Line State / Richard P. Cox.
p. cm.
Includes bibliographical references.
ISBN 978-1-59629-419-6
1. Maryland--History--Civil War, 1861-1865--Anecdotes. 2. United States--History-
-Civil War, 1861-1865--Anecdotes. 3. Maryland--History--Civil War, 1861-1865--
Biography. 4. United States--History--Civil War, 1861-1865--Biography. I. Title.
E512.C695 2008
973.7'452--dc22
2008017748

For my parents

CONTENTS

PREFACE

I want to say a few words about what this book is and what it isn't. It is a set of "stories" (really essays) about Maryland and Marylanders in the Civil War. I wanted to write about people and events I found interesting and colorful that played some significant role in the conduct or aftermath of the war, or illustrate some of its more ironic or paradoxical elements. Some of the stories tell of people and events that many readers will find familiar, and I have tried to tell them in new ways, adding lesser known facts or dispelling some of the mythology built up around them. Other stories may be relatively unfamiliar.

I have made no attempt to chronicle the entire history of Maryland's involvement in the war—that would be beyond my ability. There is no "theme" to this book, and I haven't tried to prove or disprove any particular "theory" about the war or Maryland's involvement in it. I have tried to tell the stories in an objective way and not let my biases show too much. I am not a native Marylander, so I have no axes to grind or local ancestors to brag about or vindicate—I don't have a dog in the fight, as the saying goes.

The selection of topics is a bit lopsided. The stories feature more Confederates than Unionists, more seamen than landsmen, more men than women and scarcely an African American voice is heard. I don't apologize for my selection, but I admit that I chose the topics partly because of the type of material I found.

In my reading and research about Maryland and the war, I found that until fairly recently much of the writing on Maryland Civil War history focused on Confederates or emphasized the Southern perspective. Many of the treatments of Maryland's involvement in the war focused on the Union's trampling on the rights of Maryland citizens, justifying the pro-secession position and defending Confederate war policy—variations on what scholars call the "theory of the Lost Cause." This was not too surprising, especially when one considers that until about the time of the Civil War centennial in 1961–65, Northerners had produced very little writing about the war. Bruce Catton and Shelby Foote notwithstanding, until the publication of James M. McPherson's *Battle Cry of Freedom* in 1988, very few comprehensive and scholarly treatments of the war existed that attempted a "balanced" view supported by extensive documentary evidence. McPherson discusses the reason for this in one of his recent articles.[1]

A comprehensive survey of Maryland historiography on the Civil War has yet to be written. One would certainly be welcomed. Fortunately, books that feature what people from whom we have not previously heard saw and felt about the war are beginning to appear.[2]

I am not a professional historian, but I have tried to tell these stories with as much detail and historical evidence as I could find. I would be grateful for any comments about factual errors or other ways that I have gone astray. My e-mail address is at the end of the book.

A writer once supposedly showed Dr. Samuel Johnson a copy of his new work and asked the literary celebrity for a critique. Johnson read it and replied, "Your manuscript is both good and original. But the part that is good is not original, and the part that is original is not good." I hope I have escaped a similar reproach.

ACKNOWLEDGEMENTS

No man is an island," wrote the poet John Donne, and it is true that few writers ever produced anything worthwhile without the help of others. I am deeply indebted to the many people who helped me along the path this book has taken.

Several of these essays first appeared as articles in the Civil War section of the *Washington Times*. Writing for the *Times* was enjoyable, but I came to realize how difficult it is to explore a subject in twelve hundred words when there was so much more to write. I didn't start out planning to do a book-length compendium of those articles; the idea just slowly took root as I found I had completed several articles and had ideas for many more. Many thanks to Greg Pierce, the editor of the *Times*'s Civil War page, for his encouragement and belief that I had something worthwhile to say. All of the articles originally appearing in the *Washington Times* have been revised and expanded. Other essays have been written specifically for this book.

I did most of my research in the friendly confines of the Maryland State Law Library in Annapolis and the H. Furlong Baldwin Library of the Maryland Historical Society in Baltimore. The Maryland State Law Library is much more than just a law library—it is rich in original and secondary sources on Maryland history. Both libraries have excellent and helpful staffs.

Christopher Becker and David Angerhofer of the Maryland Historical Society were extremely helpful in locating illustrations. Rob Schoeberlein, head of special collections at the Maryland State Archives, also provided much help with tracking down photographs and illustrations. My gratitude also to David Clark, whose drawing of the Zarvona incident accompanied my article in the *Washington Times* and is used here with his permission. Since no known photographs of Zarvona exist, a caricature will have to do.

Dr. Edward C. Papenfuse, Maryland state archivist, patiently answered my emails seeking additional information on the Crossland versus Mynne coat of arms controversy. William S. Dudley read an early version of the manuscript and provided many helpful comments. Thanks also to the late Harry McCrone, whose course on Maryland in the Civil War at Anne Arundel Community College gave me many interesting insights on the war from a native Marylander's perspective and filled in many gaps in my knowledge.

I also want to say something about the use of the computer for historical research. As anyone who has researched Civil War material knows, there is a staggering amount of information on the Internet. Alas, as with much Internet content, not all of the material is accurate or reliable. It is a good place to start, but that's when the real work begins. I want to acknowledge two websites I found particularly helpful in my research. The relatively new "Google Book Search" search engine is a wonderful source for locating out-of-print books or books that are too hard to obtain through interlibrary loans. And as anyone who has done research in *Official Records of the War of the Rebellion* knows, locating a complete set and using the indices can be daunting. Fortunately, the Cornell University Library has digitized the *Official Records* in both the army and navy series, and the whole set is available on the library's website. Doing research at home is always more convenient, and I heartily recommend these sites to students of the war.

INTRODUCTION

I have always been fascinated with the Civil War. I grew up in the Midwest and always wanted to see and walk the places where Americans wearing blue and gray fought each other generations before I was born. When I moved to Maryland in 1993, I was delighted to find that all the major battlefields and sites in the eastern theatre of the war that I had read about were a couple of hours' drive away. I spent as many weekends as I could immersed in the war.

One of my first forays was to the Gettysburg battlefield. As I went through the National Cemetery with tourists from all over the country, the guide pointed out how the Union dead had been interred according to their state of origin. Someone in the group, probably from the Old Line State, asked why there were so few Marylanders' graves. The guide asked how many in our group were from Maryland. About ten hands shot up. "What side did Maryland fight on in the war?" he asked. For a moment there were blank stares, and then someone blurted out, "Both!"

I knew this, of course, from my reading, but it was only after many more years of learning about the state's role in the war and talking to native Marylanders that I came to realize what that meant. Fighting on both sides of our great national conflict; with communities, even families, split down the middle; questions about whether Maryland is a Northern or a Southern state; and disagreements about the war that can still be heard 140 years after the fact—that's the part of living in Maryland I find most intriguing.

How did this statewide trauma come about? One common explanation is economics and Maryland's unique geographical position. Maryland was founded as a planter colony, and tobacco became the principal cash crop. In this, Maryland resembled Virginia more than any other colony, and strong economic and social ties grew between them as trade developed and families intermarried. Another economic factor was slavery, which entered Maryland in its earliest days. From its founding until well into the nineteenth century, Maryland was dominated by a Tidewater plantation economy based on ownership of land and slaves. Besides their land, slaves were the planters' main form of capital, amounting to millions of dollars.

Even though Maryland was below the Mason-Dixon line, and therefore in the eyes of many was part of the "upper South," the term that best describes Maryland is the "middle." Whether as one of the "middle colonies" or as a "mid-Atlantic" state, Maryland's proximity to the North meant that it would be influenced from that direction as well. And that influence would gather force as industry expanded, the railroads came and Baltimore became a major port, sending its clipper ships around the world. Newer European immigrants settled vast portions of the western part of the state and didn't grow tobacco, but grew wheat, oats and corn instead on smaller landholdings. These new Marylanders didn't want or need slaves, and they felt no kinship with the Tidewater slaveholders.

Southern Maryland and the Eastern Shore were dominated by the planter culture and were Southern in their economic, social and political leanings. The western portion of the state contained mostly small farmers, with economic and family ties closer to Pennsylvania and other parts of the North. Baltimore was a commercial city, with important connections to Northern commerce, but with many economic and social ties to the South. The city's loyalties were split. In short, Maryland on the brink of the Civil War was the "middle ground," looking both North and South.

Then came the 1860 election and the secession crisis that followed. There were four candidates for president that year. The Democrats had split into two separate factions along North-South lines and each faction ran its own candidate. The popular vote in Maryland went heavily for John Breckinridge, the Southern Democratic candidate. Abraham Lincoln received the fewest votes among the four candidates—in some Maryland counties, Lincoln received less than five votes; and in one county (Worcester), he received none.[1]

It is difficult to gauge just how strong secession feelings were in the state, since no referendum was ever held, as there had been in Virginia. Far more Marylanders ultimately fought for the North than for the South, but whether this was an expression of the sentiments of the "silent majority" or dictated by later events is hard to determine. The runner-up in the 1860 presidential popular vote in Maryland was John Bell of the Constitutional Union Party, a new party that stood for little more than the status quo. Perhaps it is fair to say that the status quo was exactly what Marylanders preferred.

But events soon moved in an ominous direction, and the status quo didn't hold. South Carolina seceded in December 1860, and the Deep South followed. Maryland, with its strong ties to Virginia, more or less waited to see what its sister state across the Potomac would do. If Virginia hadn't left the Union, secession sentiment in Maryland might have died out fairly quickly.

Soon shots were fired at Fort Sumter and Virginia seceded. The war came, causing Marylanders to take sides or attempt to remain neutral. For the duration of the war, the state would be occupied by Federal troops, sent by a government that deeply distrusted the loyalty of many Marylanders.

There is one other geographical piece of the puzzle that was probably the deciding element sealing Maryland's fate during the sectional crisis—Washington, D.C. If the nation's capital and Maryland had not been positioned between the seceding states and the North, perhaps the state's fate would have been different. But the Federal government was determined to defend Washington, whatever the cost.

And so, if one accepts the proposition that geography ultimately determined Maryland's fate, then the people most responsible for it are none other than George Washington, Alexander Hamilton, Thomas Jefferson and James Madison. Their dinner meeting in New York in June 1790, at which Jefferson and Madison agreed to Hamilton's plan for the federal government to assume the debts of the states in exchange for moving the federal capital to the banks of the Potomac, was the determining event.[2]

CASUALTIES

The despot's heal is on thy shore,
Maryland!
His torch is at thy temple door,
Maryland!
Avenge the patriotic gore
That flecked the streets of Baltimore
And be the battle queen of yore,
Maryland, My Maryland!
—James Ryder Randall, 1861

Civil wars are notoriously bloody affairs. It has been estimated that between six hundred thousand and seven hundred thousand soldiers and sailors died in America's Civil War, more than in all of its other conflicts from the War of Independence to Vietnam combined.[1] In addition, well over four hundred thousand combatants were wounded but survived. It is unlikely that we will ever know how many civilians were killed or wounded in the war.

In our own time, daily images of terrorism and all-too-familiar terms such as "collateral damage" and "body counts" have perhaps inured us to some of the horrors of war. But nineteenth-century military precepts dictated that civilian casualties should be a rarity and were not a part of "civilized" warfare. That was to change in 1861, as it had in previous internecine conflicts such as the English Civil War and the Thirty Years' War in Germany.

It has been stated so often that it is now accepted truth that the first casualties of the Civil War occurred in Maryland a few days after the fall of Fort Sumter. Common wisdom has it that the Fort Sumter bombardment produced no casualties. Yet according to the National Park Service, there were in fact casualties at Sumter. Though no one was killed or wounded during the actual bombardment on April 12–13, 1861, one Federal soldier was killed and three were wounded when a cannon exploded while firing a salute during the evacuation of the fort on April 14.[2] And there are unconfirmed reports of at least one Confederate death. Surely these casualties must be counted as a direct result of the bombardment, and therefore were Civil War casualties predating the events in Maryland.

But could a Marylander have been one of the casualties at Sumter? There is no evidence that anyone from Maryland was among the killed or wounded, but there were plenty of Marylanders in Charleston during the bombardment. After South Carolina seceded in December 1860, the state sent recruiting officers to Baltimore. They enlisted five hundred men and sent them by ship to Charleston, where they were assigned to Lucas's (Infantry) Battalion of South Carolina and Rhett's First South Carolina Artillery in Charleston Harbor. Thus, the odds are that some of those Marylanders took part in the bombardment. In addition, there were many Maryland soldiers in the Fort Sumter Federal garrison.[3]

In any event, it is an undeniable fact that the first *civilian* casualties of the war occurred in Maryland. And the events of April 18–19, 1861, in Baltimore would, in many ways, seal Maryland's fate as the secession crisis unfolded and the country slipped into war.

After Fort Sumter surrendered, Lincoln issued a "Proclamation of Insurrection" and called on the states' governors to raise seventy-five thousand ninety-day volunteer troops to reinforce Washington and assist with putting down the rebellion. This action did much to inflame anti-Union sentiment in the upper South, particularly in Virginia and Maryland, but did the president have any choice?

In 1861, the standing army of the United States consisted of only about sixteen thousand men, most of whom were stationed at faraway frontier posts west of the Mississippi or working on engineering projects around the country. The War Department knew it would take considerable time to redeploy and concentrate the regular army from hundreds of stations in the states and territories. The navy was even more scattered. Many ships and sailors were posted on land or sea duty thousands of miles away. And it was unknown how many soldiers and sailors of Southern origin were prepared to fight for the Union.[4]

The Lincoln administration also knew that if the states of the upper South (again, primarily Virginia and Maryland) seceded, the Union was in serious trouble. How would it be possible to maintain the government and rally the country to counter the rebellion if the nation's capital were completely surrounded by seceding states? There were few soldiers in Washington itself. Congress had adjourned and was not scheduled to reconvene until the fall. How could congressmen get to the capital if it were cut off from the rest of the country? And if either Virginia or Maryland—or both—left the Union, what would prevent a secessionist army from marching into Washington?

Adding to the sense of urgency was another stark reality—it would take time to mobilize the requisitioned volunteer regiments, equip them and send them on their way to the capital. And if those regiments were to arrive quickly to support the government, they would have to travel by rail. All of the railroads entering Washington from the North passed through Maryland, and all but one passed through Baltimore.

And then the other shoe dropped. On April 17, Virginia adopted an ordinance of secession. One of the commonwealth's first acts was to send militia to Harper's Ferry to seize the Federal armory with its cache of weapons and the machinery for making more. Harper's Ferry was also the point where the Baltimore and Ohio (B&O) Railroad entered Maryland from the West. Virginia's troops temporarily stopped the B&O's trains from reaching Washington.[5] Maryland secessionists had been waiting to see what action Virginia would take. Once secession became a reality in Virginia, pro-secessionist Marylanders began organizing to follow suit.

The first state to offer troops to the Lincoln administration was Minnesota, for the serendipitous reason that the state's governor happened to be in Washington when Lincoln announced his call for volunteers.[6] But Minnesota was over a thousand miles away. Clearly, if the Federal government were to survive, immediate help would have to come from loyal states closer to the capital.

On April 18, a troop of Pennsylvania volunteers entered Maryland. Approximately 550 soldiers, including the Washington Artillerists and National Light Infantry from Pottsville, had left Harrisburg and arrived in Baltimore at the Northern Central Railroad's Bolton Depot. They were poorly equipped and virtually unarmed. They marched down Howard and Pratt Streets to the B&O Railroad's Mount Clare Depot, escorted by local policemen for protection.

As the soldiers marched, a large crowd of "disorderly characters" followed, showering the troops with paving stones and brickbats. Nickoles Biddle, a free African American servant of a captain in the Washington Artillerists, was struck in the face. His cut was so severe that it exposed bone.

Biddle survived, but he bore a scar from the incident until his death in 1876. His tombstone recalled the event and bore the epitaph: "His Was the Proud Distinction of Shedding the First Blood in the Late War for the Union."[7] A free black Pennsylvanian had become the first civilian casualty of the war.

The following day, there took place what has become known in popular memory as the Pratt Street Riot. As one writer has put it, that day would see

> *the most chronicled event in the history of the city since the bombardment of Fort McHenry in 1814, and make Baltimore the first battlefield of the Civil War.*[8]

The first fully armed and equipped regiment to answer Lincoln's call was the Sixth Massachusetts Volunteer Regiment. The regiment left Boston by train on April 17. At Philadelphia, the regiment's commander was warned that Southern sympathizers in Baltimore might oppose their passage through the city. They departed for Baltimore on the eighteenth, via the Philadelphia, Wilmington and Baltimore (PW&B) Railroad, and hoped to pass through Baltimore very early on the nineteenth to avoid a confrontation with pro-Confederates. However, their passage was held up at the Susquehanna River, since at the time there was no railroad bridge spanning it. Instead, steamers carried passengers across the river and a train on the other side took them south.

At about 11:00 a.m. on the nineteenth, the Sixth Massachusetts, along with seven companies of unarmed Pennsylvania volunteers, arrived in Baltimore at the PW&B's President Street Depot east of the Inner

Pratt Street Riot, Baltimore, April 19, 1861. *Courtesy of the Maryland Historical Society.*

Harbor. The passenger cars, with the soldiers aboard, then had to be transported to the B&O's Camden Street Station, about a mile to the west, where that railroad's cars would take them to Washington.

Why all this moving about from depot to depot? In the early days of railroading, there were no "union" stations that served as terminals for all the railroads entering a city. In 1861, four railroads had service to Baltimore: the B&O; the PW&B; the Northern Central and the Western Maryland. Each line had its own terminal, and passengers and goods traveling onward had to be transferred from one station to another. Adding to this complicated arrangement was a Baltimore city ordinance that prohibited locomotives on the city streets. Train engines threw off sparks, the city fathers said, that were a fire hazard. Moreover, the trains emitted noise and soot, both of which were deemed public nuisances.

And so the Massachusetts and Pennsylvania men set out for Camden Station. Teams of four horses pulled each railroad car along tracks through the city streets. The cars set out north along President Street and turned left into Pratt Street.

The first nine cars made the journey without incident. The tenth car stopped because of mechanical difficulties. The driver reversed the horse team and the car headed back to the President Street Station. By that time, a crowd had gathered, jeering and waiving secessionist flags, and people began to throw rocks at the car. Some in the crowd blocked the tracks along Pratt Street with anchors and stones from a construction site so no further cars could pass.

Neither Baltimore Mayor George Brown nor Police Marshall George Kane had been informed that the soldiers were coming until about an hour before their arrival. They struggled to keep order as the angry crowd grew. Mayor Brown was in the lead as the troops remaining at the President Street Station left for Camden Station by foot. The police tried to protect the rear of the column, but locals continued to pelt the troops with bricks and stones. When members of the crowd, by that time close to two thousand in number, blocked the march along Pratt Street, one of the officers gave the order to open fire. Many people fled, some were cut down by the bullets and others returned fire. When the troops finally reached Camden Station, they continued to fire their muskets from the B&O's railroad cars, and at least one more person was killed. A total of four soldiers were killed and thirty-six were wounded. Twelve Baltimoreans lay dead and an unknown number had been wounded.[9]

One romantic legend about the Pratt Street Riot is that the Sixth Massachusetts troops were descendants of the minutemen, who had fought another famous battle on another April 19—at Lexington and Concord in

President Street Station, Baltimore, as it appears today.

1775. Like their forebears, they had fired "shots heard around the world." In fact, the men of the Sixth came from the considerably less romantic factory and mill towns of Lowell and Lawrence.

When the Sixth Massachusetts finally arrived in Washington, two women from their native state came to the station to care for the wounded and took some of the serious cases into their home. They were Sally Vassal and her sister, a clerk in the U.S. Patent Office named Clara Barton. Thus began the nursing career of the "Angel of the Battlefield." Clara Barton would go on to care for thousands of Civil War casualties and would later found the American Red Cross.

Hard on the heels of the Sixth Massachusetts was the Eighth Massachusetts, under the command of Benjamin Butler. Butler led his regiment into Philadelphia on the evening of April 19, where he heard about the events in Baltimore earlier in the day. He got word the next morning that Marylanders had burned the railroad bridges north of the city.

A lawyer, politician and a War Democrat, Benjamin Butler had a tarnished reputation before the war, which grew even more tarnished before the war ended. Something of a gadfly, he had supported Jefferson Davis for the Democratic Party presidential nomination in 1860. Although his later military career would be undistinguished at best, the foresight and initiative Butler showed in April and May 1861 were remarkable.

Butler took the Eighth Massachusetts to the banks of the Susquehanna River by rail. He then commandeered a steamer (appropriately named the *Maryland*) that ferried passengers across the river. Butler ordered the steamer to sail to Annapolis, where it landed at the naval academy. Within days, Butler had repaired the Annapolis and Elkridge's tracks and a locomotive (one of his soldiers had worked in the Massachusetts shop where the locomotive had been built) and reached Annapolis Junction, south of Relay, where secessionist militia had been posted to intercept him. The Seventh New York, which had followed Butler into Annapolis, entered Washington via the B&O Railroad, and the capital was temporarily secure.

Fearing that the naval academy was vulnerable to attack from Virginia and Maryland militia, Federal authorities ordered that the academy be moved to Newport, Rhode Island, for the duration of the war. On April 24, the midshipmen and instructors boarded "Old Ironsides," the USS *Constitution* (then a training ship at the academy), and the ship was towed into the Chesapeake, bound for Newport.

By mid-May, Butler had occupied Relay and had marched on Baltimore. He mounted his artillery pieces on Federal Hill and trained them on the city. Federal General in Chief Winfield Scott was outraged that Butler had occupied Baltimore without orders, and he relieved Butler

Camden Street Station, Baltimore, as it appears today.

soon after. Nevertheless, Baltimore remained an occupied city for the entire war. Butler, a political commander acting on his own initiative, probably saved Maryland for the Union. He had a plan and acted on it—the pro-secessionists had no plan and seemed to be merely reacting to events.

The events in Maryland in the spring of 1861 were far from the last time railroads would be instrumental in the war. In fact, the Civil War was the first conflict in which railroads played any kind of role. The Bolton Depot became the B&O Railroad's Mount Royal Station in 1896 and is today part of the Maryland Institute College of Art. The President Street Depot still stands. Finished in 1849, it is one of the oldest surviving train stations in the country. Until recently, it was the site of the Baltimore Civil War Museum, which vividly depicted the events of April 18–19, 1861. Sadly, as of this writing, the museum is closed due to lack of funds and the building is for sale. The Camden Street Station also survives and stands in the shadow of Oriole Park at Camden Yards. It is presently the home of Sports Legends at Camden Yards and Geppi's Entertainment Museum.

What would have happened if the Federals had decided to fight their way through Baltimore to Washington? Would more battles with pro-secessionists have so inflamed public opinion that Maryland would have seceded? If the state had seceded, would some of the battles that devastated Virginia have been fought in and laid waste to Maryland? Lying on the periphery of the Confederacy, would Maryland have been able to keep the Federals out? Would Washington have been forced to capitulate to a Confederate Maryland or Virginia? Any number of "what ifs" might have led to different outcomes for the state and nation.

Exact numbers are hard to arrive at, but it has been estimated that around sixty thousand Marylanders fought for the Union and between twenty-five thousand and thirty thousand fought for the Confederacy.[10] Extrapolating from figures for the war as a whole, perhaps as many as 15 percent of the Marylanders fighting in the war died on the battlefield or from disease. The total number of wounded is unknown.

It has also been argued that the state as a whole became a casualty of the war. Military occupation, martial law, the arrest and confinement of many leading citizens and the "taking" of millions of dollars worth of "property" in the form of slaves following emancipation—all these factors rendered Maryland a "victim" of the war every bit as much as they had the seceding and fellow border states. The Civil War was our great national tragedy, and it should not be forgotten that the nation that emerged from the struggle was forged at a very high price.

EX PARTE MERRYMAN

The extent of the president's constitutional war powers, a topic straight out of today's headlines, was no less an issue during the Civil War. An incident in Maryland very early in the crisis resulted in a clash between President Lincoln and the chief justice of the United States—a dispute that has echoes in our own time.

After the so-called Pratt Street Riot on April 19, 1861, Baltimore's Mayor George W. Brown and Governor Thomas Holliday Hicks declared that they would allow no further Northern troop transfers through the city and state. Local militias were ordered to take steps to prevent further troop movements. Militia units cut telegraph lines and destroyed bridges to deter Northern troops from passing through the state.

On the same day as the riot, President Lincoln wrote Attorney General Edward Bates, requesting an opinion on the legality of suspending the writ of habeas corpus. Not waiting for Bates's formal legal opinion, on April 27 the president authorized General in Chief Winfield Scott to suspend habeas corpus "between Washington and Maine." In reality, Lincoln intended the suspension to apply only within the vicinity of the "military line" (the railroad lines between Philadelphia and Washington) so troops wouldn't be prevented from reaching the capital. Scott delegated that authority to local commanders to use at their discretion.

Lincoln believed the capital and the nation were in imminent danger and vulnerable to attack. He justified the suspension of habeas corpus on the grounds of military necessity and took the action himself as "commander in chief" because Congress was not in session.

The suspension was at first kept secret. Even by May, after several members of the Maryland General Assembly, newspaper publishers and other prominent citizens thought to be Confederate sympathizers had been arrested without warrants or formal charges, the Federal government still had not publicly acknowledged the suspension.

After General Benjamin Butler's troops landed at Annapolis and occupied Baltimore and the B&O Railroad line into Washington, Federal troops began to pass into Washington unimpeded. With the capital temporarily secure, some Federal commanders decided it was time to round up Marylanders whom they believed had impeded their passage through the state or whom they considered disloyal to the Union.

John Merryman, a Baltimore County Democrat, state legislator, president of the Maryland State Agricultural Society and a lieutenant in the Baltimore County Horse Guards (a local militia unit), had participated in preventing some Pennsylvania troops from reaching Baltimore. He had also ordered his troops to burn a bridge over the Gunpowder River near Parkton, about ten miles from the Pennsylvania border. In the early hours of May 25, 1861, Federal troops entered "Hayfields," Merryman's home near Cockeysville, rousted him from his bed, arrested him and imprisoned him at Fort McHenry. He was given access to his attorney, who immediately filed a petition for a writ of habeas corpus.

The writ of habeas corpus, also known as the "Great Writ," is a legal proceeding by which a person held in custody can challenge the legality of his detention. The term "habeas corpus" comes from the opening words of a fourteenth-century English legal writ (a summons). The words are Latin for "[we command] that you should have the body [brought before us]" and the writ demands that the custodian of a prisoner bring the prisoner before a court to determine if he or she is being legally detained. If the court determines that there is a sufficient legal basis for the detention, the prisoner may continue to be confined; if not, the prisoner will be released.

The right to petition for a writ of habeas corpus is a long-standing tradition under English and American law. It is considered one of the most important instruments for safeguarding individual freedom against arbitrary government action. As one commentator put it, the writ

> *is the great remedy of the citizen or subject against arbitrary or illegal imprisonment; it is the mode by which the judicial power speedily and effectually protects the personal liberty of every individual, and repels the injustice of unconstitutional laws or despotic governors.*[1]

Merryman's petition was filed with the local federal circuit court. Fortunately for him, the "circuit judge" who received the petition was none other than Roger Brooke Taney, chief justice of the United States.

John Merryman. *Courtesy of the Maryland Historical Society.*

Supreme Court justices at that time served as presiding judges on the various federal circuit courts and heard cases as circuit court judges when the Supreme Court was not in session. Each of the justices was assigned to one of the geographical circuits around the country, usually near where they had their permanent homes, a practice known as "circuit riding." Taney had his permanent home in Baltimore, and was the presiding judge for the Circuit Court of Maryland.

Taney was no mere disinterested jurist when Merryman's petition came before him. He was born in 1777 on a plantation overlooking the Patuxent River. As a second son, he did not stand to inherit his father's estate, so he prepared to enter a profession. Taney was class valedictorian at Dickinson College in Pennsylvania and then read law with a judge in Annapolis. He was admitted to the Maryland bar in 1799.

After a brief legal career in Annapolis, Taney moved to Frederick, where he married Anne Key, the sister of his law partner Francis Scott Key. As a practicing attorney, Taney gained a reputation as an opponent of slavery, highlighted by his 1819 successful defense of an abolitionist preacher charged with sedition. He had freed his own slaves. Yet as a member of the Maryland planter aristocracy, Taney did not believe in the forcible elimination of slavery. Rather, he thought slavery could only be ended by each sovereign state legislating its own solution.

In 1823, Taney left Frederick to open a law office in Baltimore. A Jacksonian Democrat, Taney was appointed attorney general of Maryland in 1827 and became Andrew Jackson's attorney general in 1831. Taney succeeded John Marshall as chief justice in 1836.

The Francis Scott Key–Roger B. Taney law office in Frederick.

As a loyal Democrat, Taney was certainly no friend of the recently elected Lincoln administration. More ominously, he was also the author of the notorious *Dred Scott v. Sanford*[2] decision, which held that slaves and free descendants of slaves were "inferior beings," not citizens of the United States and that the "black man has no rights a white man is bound to respect."

There is some support for the notion that Taney's sweeping language in *Dred Scott* may have been a preemptive effort to avoid a war over the issue of slavery. By declaring once and for all that the Constitution did not and could not prohibit the institution, Taney and his colleagues may have hoped to settle the slavery issue on purely judicial grounds. But his opinion went too far. While it can be conceded that the Constitution did not expressly prohibit slavery, Taney's statement that even free blacks had no rights under federal or state law was clearly wrong (as two dissenting justices pointed out), and it so inflamed Northern public opinion that his decision had exactly the opposite effect—it made an armed conflict perhaps even more likely.

On May 26, Taney issued the writ, ordering General George Cadwalader, commander at Fort McHenry, to appear before him and deliver Merryman to the circuit courtroom on the morning of the twenty-seventh. Cadwalader did not appear; nor did Merryman. The general had sent a colonel with a statement Cadwalader had prepared reporting that President Lincoln had authorized the action seizing Merryman and that the president had suspended the writ of habeas corpus to protect the public safety. Taney was not satisfied. He issued a second writ demanding that Cadwalader produce Merryman the next day. On the twenty-eighth, a federal marshal announced to the chief justice that he had tried to serve the writ but had been detained at the outer gate at Fort McHenry. He had sent in his name, but had been told there was no answer.

Taney set to work to deal with the standoff. His opinion in the case, which became known as *Ex parte Merryman*,[3] held that Lincoln's suspension of habeas corpus was unconstitutional and beyond the powers of the president. The power to suspend the writ is set forth in Article I, section 9, clause 2 of the Constitution. Since the power to suspend the writ is contained in Article I, and since that article deals solely with the powers of Congress, Taney held that only Congress has the power to suspend habeas corpus, and only then in "cases of rebellion or invasion" where "the public safety may require it."

Taney knew that Lincoln was aware of the constitutional provision and was actually making an "argument from necessity" in defense of the government while Congress was absent. He dealt with that issue as well. Taney angrily wrote that none of the kings of England had exercised such

Chief Justice of the United States Roger Brooke Taney. *Courtesy of the Maryland State Archives.*

power, and therefore Lincoln's act was more tyrannical and despotic than any British monarch's had been. He concluded his opinion with these words:

> These great and fundamental laws...have been disregarded and suspended...by a military order, supported by force of arms. Such is the case before me, and I can only say that if the authority which the constitution has confided to the judiciary department and judicial officers, may thus, upon any pretext or under any circumstances, be usurped by the military power, at its discretion, the people of the United States are no longer living under a government of laws, but every citizen holds life, liberty and property at the will and pleasure of the army officer in whose military district he may happen to be found.[4]

Taney thought that his ruling in *Merryman* would probably lead to his arrest, and there is some evidence that Lincoln may have ordered that an arrest warrant be drawn up but later decided not to have it executed. Taney was eighty-four when he wrote the *Merryman* decision, and he had said to his friend Mayor Brown of Baltimore, "I am an old man, a very old man, but perhaps I have been preserved for this occasion."[5] His opinion in *Merryman* did much to rehabilitate his reputation as a jurist after the *Dred Scott* decision. Taney died in 1864 and Salmon P. Chase, secretary of the treasury, succeeded him as chief justice.

On July 5, Attorney General Bates finally weighed in with his formal opinion on the legality of suspending the writ. Not surprisingly, he found that the president had the power to do so. Bates wrote that

> the President must of necessity be the sole judge both of the exigency which requires him to act and of the manner in which to employ the powers intrusted [sic] to him...to discharge his constitutional and legal duty—that is, to suppress the insurrection and execute the laws...The whole subject matter is political and not judicial. The insurrection itself is purely political... The judiciary department has no legal powers [in this instance] and therefore...no court or judge can take cognizance of the political acts of the President or undertake to revise and reverse his political decisions.[6]

Bates's opinion is an early example of the constitutional doctrine that the federal courts have no jurisdiction to decide "political questions."[7]

Buoyed by Bates's opinion, Lincoln reacted to *Ex parte Merryman* by ignoring it. Ironically, Lincoln also cited as precedent for sidestepping Taney's opinion none other than Andrew Jackson, Taney's political patron, who had also ignored Supreme Court decisions because he did not believe they were binding on the executive. Lincoln could also plausibly argue that Taney wrote his decision in his capacity as a circuit court judge; thus, the *Merryman* decision was not Supreme Court precedent. But this interpretation is tenuous, since Taney explicitly wrote that "a writ of habeas corpus was filed by the Chief Justice of the United States, sitting at chambers." He ordered the case to be filed in the "Circuit Court for the District of Maryland." If he were sitting as a circuit court judge, there would be no need to order that the decision be filed in Baltimore.

In a July 1861 address to a reassembled Congress called into special session, Lincoln did seek formal authority to suspend the writ. He asked rhetorically, "Are all the laws, but one, to go unexecuted, and the government itself go to pieces, lest that one be violated?" But Congress failed to act.

Lincoln continued making unauthorized suspensions of the writ to deal with Southern sympathizers and antiwar activists in various parts of the country, and some federal courts backed Taney's ruling. Lincoln also imposed martial law in the border states of Maryland, Kentucky and Missouri. In another act that sounds eerily contemporary, trials of persons rounded up and detained were to be conducted by military commissions, although few trials actually took place.

Suspending habeas corpus and imposing martial law in the border states were extremely unpopular acts and they became contributing causes, along with the announcement of the Emancipation Proclamation, to the loss of Republican seats in the 1862 congressional elections and the resurgence of the Democrats during the 1864 election campaign.

But the government continued to justify the measures as dictated by the necessities of war. Lincoln maintained that the government was not conducting a "star chamber." After the initial roundup of alleged pro-Confederates in Maryland, all other arrests had been made public and were widely reported in the press.

When the dust settled in Maryland, John Merryman was released on bail in July 1861 and never faced trial. All charges against him were finally dropped in 1867. Merryman later served as state treasurer and once again in the Maryland General Assembly.

Other Marylanders were not so lucky. It has been estimated that well over one hundred Marylanders were arrested and confined for much longer periods—many in military posts out of the state—and deprived of the ability to challenge their detention. Their number included Mayor Brown of Baltimore, the city police chief and police commissioner, thirty-one members of the General Assembly and congressmen, judges and newspaper editors.[8]

On February 14, 1862, Lincoln ordered that all military prisoners be released on parole and granted them amnesty for past alleged offenses on condition of their taking an oath of allegiance to the United States. Congress finally enacted the Habeas Corpus Act of 1863, formally granting the president the power to suspend the writ for the duration of the war.

In 1866, the Supreme Court ruled on the suspension of habeas corpus in another famous case, *Ex parte Milligan*.[9] Since the petitioner in that case had been denied the writ after Congress had authorized suspension, the court (now absent Taney) conceded that there were situations in which suspension could be justified during the "late wicked Rebellion." The court noted that the 1863 act was explicit as to the conditions for suspension, and that the public safety demanded that the president under those circumstances not be required to give the cause of detention by being answerable under the writ.

> *But it is not contemplated that* [a] *person should be detained…beyond a certain fixed period, unless certain judicial proceedings…were commenced against him.*[10]

Moreover, military trials in areas where the civil courts were capable of functioning were unconstitutional.[11]

Lest anyone think that the exigencies of war played out any differently in the South, it should be noted that Jefferson Davis also suspended habeas corpus in various parts of the Confederacy. Davis secured his authority from the Confederate Congress under a provision of the Confederate Constitution that was identical to Article I, section 9, clause 2 of the U.S. Constitution. Confederate legislators approved suspension of the writ to quell civil disorder and to enforce the Draft Act of 1862, which extended all twelve-month military enlistments for the duration of the war.

The Confederate Congress did, however, place severe limits and conditions on suspending habeas corpus. The legislation also contained a "sunset" provision, mandating its expiration unless Congress renewed it. Davis used his authority sparingly, and suspension of the writ lasted only about sixteen months.[12] However, many states' rights advocates considered suspension of the writ a step toward despotism. Extreme states' rights advocate Governor Joseph E. Brown of Georgia inveighed against the measure, and in 1864 the Georgia Assembly declared suspension of the writ unconstitutional.[13]

At least Davis didn't have to deal with an "interfering" judiciary. The Confederate Constitution authorized a supreme court, but the court never came into existence. Confederate legislators could not agree on how broad the powers of a supreme court should be or even whether a court was necessary. States' rights advocates feared a powerful Confederate court system would exercise the same sort of "tyranny" they believed the U.S. federal courts had exercised over the states. Some lower "national" district courts did exist, but Confederate courts had no jurisdiction to hear appeals from state courts. Even the Confederate government preferred to prosecute most of its cases in state courts on the theory that state court judgments would have greater respect.[14] Court challenges to suspension of the writ did occur, most often from deserters and other persons held in military captivity. Nevertheless, every state supreme court and Confederate district court sustained the constitutionality of compulsory military service and declined to grant writs of habeas corpus.[15]

An ancient legal maxim from Cicero states: *inter arma silent leges* (Latin for "during war, the laws are silent"). That adage does not seem to have much currency in the United States, however. As recent events have shown, our courts have always grappled—and continue to grapple—with difficult questions of how and under what conditions we are to maintain the rule of law even when the nation is faced with internal and external danger.

Issues and legal disputes arising during the Civil War, including the tension between civil liberties and the perceived requirements of national security, resonate in our own era. Perhaps it is comforting to know that both *Ex parte Merryman* and *Ex parte Milligan* have been reaffirmed and cited with approval in *Hamdi v. Rumsfeld*[16] and *Hamdan v. Rumsfeld*,[17] two recent Supreme Court cases dealing with the rule of law in an age of terrorism.

BROTHER AGAINST BROTHER

A historical marker outside Front Royal, Virginia, bears the inscription "Brother Against Brother," and that overused expression was never truer than on May 23, 1862, when the First Maryland Regiment (CSA) met and routed the First Maryland Regiment (USA). It would become the first of several battles in which Marylanders fought and killed each other during the war.

Several Maryland militia members and other volunteers went South even before shots were fired at Fort Sumter. Others waited to see whether Maryland would secede. Governor Thomas Holliday Hicks was an Eastern Shore slaveholder but a Unionist. He tried to buy time by urging the Lincoln administration to refrain from sending Northern troops through the state or take any other action that would inflame pro-secession sentiment in Maryland.

On April 26, 1861, the Maryland General Assembly met in Frederick to consider the issue of secession. The assembly met in Frederick because Annapolis had been occupied by Federal troops and was under martial law. Governor Hicks had put off calling a special session of the General Assembly to delay a vote on secession. He thought Frederick was a better place to meet because that part of the state was known to be anti-secessionist. The General Assembly did not vote for secession, opting instead to send delegations to Lincoln and the Confederate government to plead for a peaceful solution.

When the General Assembly met on June 4, it tried to have it both ways—it pronounced secession to be unconstitutional, but it also condemned the federal government for "coercing" the Southern states into taking radical action, instituting martial law and arbitrarily arresting citizens. The delegates also agreed not to allow Federal troops to pass through the state.

But the assembly's attempt to remain neutral was moot, since Federal troops already occupied Annapolis, Baltimore and key points along the Baltimore and Ohio Railroad. When the General Assembly tried to meet in September, more than thirty-one delegates who were thought to be pro-Confederate were arrested. When it met on September 17, the assembly lacked a quorum and had to adjourn.

Realizing that Maryland would not secede (or perhaps more accurately would not be allowed to secede), several thousand Marylanders crossed the Potomac and enlisted in Confederate regiments in Virginia and North Carolina. About eight hundred men, mainly militia from in and around Baltimore, formed the Maryland Battalion at Harper's Ferry. When Virginia's troops were transferred to the Confederate army, the Maryland Battalion was renamed the First Maryland Infantry Regiment.

The regiment fought gallantly at First Bull Run (Manassas). In early 1862, the Marylanders were assigned to Richard Ewell, whose troops were soon dispatched to join Stonewall Jackson in the Shenandoah Valley.

Governor Hicks, again trying to buy time, did not immediately respond to Lincoln's call for volunteers to help put down the rebellion.

Kemp Hall in Frederick, where the Maryland General Assembly met to consider secession in 1861.

Nevertheless, a number of loyal citizens of Baltimore, Ellicott Mills and Frederick began to organize, led by John R. Kenly, brigadier general of the Third Brigade, Maryland Militia.[1] Hicks issued a proclamation on May 14 calling for three-month volunteers. Lincoln issued a second request for troops on May 2, this time asking for three-year enlistments. A recruiting office was opened in Baltimore.[2]

The Federal First Maryland was mustered into service on May 27, 1861, at Washington Junction along the B&O line, and John Kenly became colonel of the regiment. One of the regiment's first assignments was to march to Baltimore to arrest Police Marshall Kane and take control of the city's police department. The regiment was then assigned to guard duty along the Maryland side of the Potomac River and the Chesapeake and Ohio (C&O) Canal between Hancock and Cumberland, and several companies saw action against Confederate raiding parties. The regiment also helped to extricate stranded Federal units after the disaster at Ball's Bluff near Leesburg, Virginia, in October 1861. In March 1862, the regiment crossed into Virginia with General Nathaniel Bank's troops and moved into the Shenandoah Valley.

Banks was inching up from Winchester to locate Jackson and give him battle. The main Federal force was at Strasburg and the lead element, the First Maryland, was at Front Royal. By May 22, Jackson was marching north down the Luray Valley with Ewell in the lead. On the morning of the twenty-third, as Ewell approached Front Royal, he received a report that the Federal First Maryland was holding the town.

Ewell sent for the Confederate First Maryland, which was at the rear of his column. The Confederate Marylanders had been itching to meet their Federal counterparts, the "bogus" First Maryland as they called it, and now they had been assigned the place of honor—they would lead the attack.

What happened next became a classic episode in the annals of the war. One of the Confederacy's most famous female spies—Belle Boyd, "the Cleopatra of the Secession"—happened to be in Front Royal. Originally from Martinsburg, Virginia (now West Virginia), Belle's earlier spying had landed her in Federal confinement in Baltimore. She had recently been released and was staying with relatives in Front Royal.

Boyd had been gathering all the intelligence she could about the size and disposition of Banks's force, but she had no way to report it to Jackson. Suddenly, Federal troops were running about and shouting that the Rebels were coming. She ran to a second-story balcony and saw, through opera glasses, the Confederate advance guard about three-quarters of a mile from the town.

FRONT ROYAL, VIRGINIA, LOOKING

Front Royal, Virginia, during the Civil War, from *Harper's Weekly*. *Courtesy of the Maryland State Archives.*

I.—Sketched by C. L. B.—[See Page 411.]

Boyd ran to meet the column. Her sense of urgency was heightened by the knowledge that her father was serving with Jackson's army. Yankee pickets fired at her and an artillery shell barely missed her. She made it to the Confederate line and saw an officer she knew, Marylander Henry Kyd Douglas. She reported to Douglas that the town was full of Yankees but the force was very small—one regiment of Maryland infantry, several pieces of artillery and a few companies of cavalry.

> *Tell him* [Jackson] *I know, for I went through the camps and got it from an officer. Tell him to charge right now and he will catch them all.*[3]

She gave Douglas the disposition of the artillery covering the bridges "like a staff officer making a report." She also said that Banks was twenty miles away in Strasburg and Banks believed Jackson was miles away in Harrisonburg. Douglas immediately reported to Jackson, who rode forward and offered Boyd an escort and transportation back to town. She declined, saying she would go back the way she came. Her parting words were: "My love to all the dear boys, and remember—if you meet me in town later you haven't seen me today." She then nonchalantly walked back toward Front Royal, waving her bonnet.[4]

The Confederate Marylanders and some Louisiana troops quickly drove in the Yankee pickets and swarmed through the town. The Federal Marylanders put up a stiff resistance. Front Royal became one of the few Civil War battles that was fought, for a time, building-by-building and street-by-street.

The Confederates advanced through Front Royal and the Federal Marylanders attempted to hold them off on a hill near a river crossing. Discovering that Confederate cavalry was approaching from the west, the Federals retreated across the bridges of the north and south forks of the Shenandoah River and attempted to burn them. The Confederates ran forward to douse the flames and saved the bridges.

The Federals withdrew beyond Cedarville with the Confederate cavalry in close pursuit. When the Federal Marylanders finally turned to make a stand, the Rebel cavalry swept around their flanks. Colonel Kenly fell severely wounded and the defense collapsed. The balance of the Federals threw down their weapons and surrendered.

After the battle, Marylanders on both sides lived out the "brother against brother" theme. As a historian of the Confederate First Maryland put it, when Colonel Kenly and the Maryland prisoners of war were brought into town, their fellow Marylanders met them, and *in many instances neighbors recognized and greeted neighbors, in some cases brothers met again with brothers, as victors and vanquished in the "fortunes of war."*[5]

Badly outnumbered at Front Royal, the Federal Marylanders' casualties were 14 killed, 43 wounded and 535 captured.[6] But their gallant defense gave Banks time to withdraw his small force from the Shenandoah Valley in safety.

These two "Firsts" never met in battle again. The Federal prisoners were sent to Richmond, paroled in September and declared exchanged two months later. Most rejoined the regiment, which in the meantime had been assigned to the Maryland Brigade of the Eighth Corps. In March 1864, when their three-year enlistments were up, the regiment reenlisted almost to a man and was assigned to the Fifth Corps, where it fought many battles as part of the Army of the Potomac until Appomattox.

After winning the "Battle of Maryland" at Front Royal, the Confederate First Maryland saw plenty of action during the remainder of Jackson's 1862 Valley Campaign and fought bravely during the Seven Days around Richmond. But their fate became entangled with the fortunes of war.

The regiment's enlistment period expired just before Second Bull Run (Manassas). Some had hopes of forming a new Maryland regiment. Having crossed the Potomac, they knew they couldn't go home. They had attached themselves to the Confederacy for the duration of the war.

A new First Maryland was formed, but was soon re-designated the Second Maryland Battalion to distinguish it from its predecessor. In June 1863, at the start of Robert E. Lee's second invasion of the North, the Second fought another "Battle of Maryland" by driving the Federal Fifth Maryland out of Winchester, Virginia. One of the Confederate captains captured his brother there, a surgeon in the Federal unit.

The Second fought yet another "Battle of Maryland" at Gettysburg on the morning of July 3, 1863. At Culp's Hill, they engaged the Federal First Maryland Eastern Shore Infantry. Color Sergeant Robert Ross of the Federal regiment was a cousin of Color Sergeant P.M. Moore of the Confederate regiment, who was wounded and captured by one of his Eastern Shore neighbors.[7] As Colonel Wallace of the Federal regiment wrote,

The 1st [Second] Maryland Confederate Regiment met us and were cut to pieces. We sorrowfully gathered up many of our old friends and acquaintances and had them carefully and tenderly cared for.[8]

The Federal First Maryland Eastern Shore had been enlisted as a home guard regiment. When it was ordered to Baltimore to join the Army of the Potomac before the Gettysburg campaign, the soldiers of Company K, from heavily pro-Confederate Somerset and Worcester Counties, reminded army authorities of the terms of their enlistment and refused to go. On July 2, as their comrades were taking positions on Culp's Hill, sixty-seven members of Company K were disarmed, dishonorably discharged and given train fare back to Salisbury.

The Confederate Marylanders suffered nearly 50 percent casualties at Gettysburg. A monument to their gallantry was erected on Culp's Hill in 1884. It was the first Confederate monument erected on the Gettysburg battlefield, and it stirred a good deal of controversy at the time. The Second remained with Lee's army to the end. At Appomattox, the regiment could muster only sixty-three men.[9]

The historical record does not show whether the Confederate and Union Marylanders got together again during the surrender at Appomattox. We can only hope that they did, and that the good feelings expressed after their meeting at Front Royal and other fields of conflict continued and grew deeper as the war ended and their home state, and the nation, began to heal.

MARYLAND'S CONFEDERATE ADMIRALS

In a war that abounded with irony, one of the supreme ironies is that Maryland remained in the Union yet produced the only Confederate naval officers who attained the rank of admiral. Franklin Buchanan became the Confederacy's highest-ranking naval officer and Raphael Semmes became its most famous naval hero.

The Confederate navy was top-heavy with Marylanders. In addition to the only 2 admirals, Maryland furnished a commodore, 7 captains, 4 commanders, 7 lieutenants commanding vessels or shore batteries and 15 other lieutenants. In total, 163 documented Marylanders served as officers in the relatively small Confederate navy.[1]

FRANKLIN BUCHANAN

Franklin Buchanan was one of the most illustrious officers in the U.S. Navy. He was born in Baltimore in 1800 and joined the navy as a midshipman in 1815. Over the four and a half decades of his U.S. Naval career, Buchanan saw more extensive and worldwide sea duty than any other officer. He was one of the senior officers who lobbied strenuously for a better officer-training program, and he became the first superintendent of the U.S. Naval Academy when it opened in 1845. Buchanan served during the Mexican War and accompanied Admiral Perry on his groundbreaking expedition to Japan. Just prior to the Civil War, he was a senior captain and commandant of the Washington Navy Yard.

Most U.S. Naval officers who joined the Confederate navy simply resigned their commissions. But the Federal Navy Department, no doubt thinking them traitors, refused to accept their resignations. Instead, their

Admiral Franklin Buchanan, Confederate States Navy. *Courtesy of the U.S. Naval Historical Center.*

names were struck from the roll of active officers and they were marked down as dismissed.

This situation caused no little embarrassment for Buchanan, who was one of the most senior members of the Federal service. Incensed by the Pratt Street Riot and disturbed by the U.S. Navy Department's hasty preparations for war, on April 22 Buchanan walked into Secretary of the Navy Gideon Welles's office and handed in his resignation.

Believing that Maryland was certain to secede, Buchanan retreated to "the Rest," his home in Talbot County, to await the unfolding of events. Within a few days, however, he began to regret his hasty resignation. Maryland did not secede, nor did it seem likely that Federal authorities would allow her to do so. Buchanan wrote to Gideon Welles on May 4, indicating that he wanted to rescind his resignation. He wrote to a friend the same day that he regretted resigning, was not a secessionist and that he would be unhappy out of the service. But Welles curtly replied that his name had been struck from the navy list.

Other Maryland naval officers received similar treatment, in one case with tragic consequences. Commodore Isaac Mayo was a fifty-two-year veteran of the U.S. Navy. Mayo owned an estate in Anne Arundel County (the city of Mayo and the Mayo Peninsula are named after him), and he was the driving force in securing Annapolis as the site of the U.S. Naval Academy. Among his extensive sea duties was service as commander of the U.S. Navy's African Squadron, where he had commanded the USS *Constitution* ("Old Ironsides") in government efforts to interdict slave ships bound for the United States from West Africa.

Mayo submitted his resignation one week after Buchanan's, writing that he protested "in the name of humanity against this 'war against brethren.' I cannot fight against the Constitution while pretending to fight for it."[2] Welles sent him a short note informing him that he had been dismissed. Welles believed that officers who would not stand by the Union in the present crisis were not to be trusted with a commission. Denied the honor of resigning, Mayo promptly died under mysterious circumstances. In all probability he committed suicide.[3]

Buchanan was shocked and angered by his treatment. He wrote a letter to a nephew in Baltimore that seemed to reflect the sentiments of Governor Hicks and many other Marylanders ambivalently struggling to deal with events that were overwhelming them.

> *I am as strong a Union man as any in the country. I am no secessionist. I do not admit the right of secession, but at the same time I admit the right of revolution…My intention is to remain neutral. But if all law is to be dispensed with…and a coercive policy continued which would disgust barbarians, and the South literally trampled upon, I may change my mind and join them.*[4]

Very soon, however, events that personally affected Buchanan turned him irrevocably toward the Confederacy. In June, Federal soldiers landed at his private dock and occupied Easton, removing arms and ammunition from the armory. Then some of the soldiers tried to remove decorative cannonballs from the gateposts at Buchanan's home, which he had captured from a fort during the Mexican War. A confrontation took place, and the Federal officer in charge reluctantly ordered his men to replace the cannonballs, but two could not be found.

Soon after this incident, Buchanan clandestinely wrote to Richmond inquiring if his services would be useful and what rank he could expect to receive. He learned from his contacts that it was Confederate policy to grant former U.S. naval officers the same rank and pay they had previously attained. Buoyed by this information, toward the end of August 1861 he went to the Talbot County courthouse in Easton and transferred all of his property to his wife and children. If the Federals deemed him a traitor and tried to confiscate his property, they would find that he legally owned nothing.

In 1835, Buchanan had married Ann Catherine (Nannie) Lloyd, the daughter of former governor, congressman and U.S. senator Edward Lloyd. Colonel Lloyd (as he was known from his days in the Maryland militia) saw slavery as a positive social blessing. In 1807, as a congressman, he had been one of the few to vote against the termination of the international slave trade, despite its mandatory suspension in 1808 as the U.S. Constitution required. He had also opposed the Missouri Compromise because of its ban on slavery in the Louisiana Territory north of the Missouri boundary.

Lloyd was the master of Wye House, one of the largest plantations on the Eastern Shore, as well as several other properties, and the owner of hundreds of slaves. Frederick Douglass, whose slave master was an overseer on one of Lloyd's farms, was a frequent visitor at Wye House during the time Buchanan courted Nannie. Douglass had much to say about Colonel Lloyd and the Talbot County plantation culture in his 1845 autobiography, *The Narrative of the Life of Frederick Douglass, an American Slave*.

Having married into the Eastern Shore planter aristocracy, it would have been extraordinary for Buchanan to have maintained his "neutrality" while virtually every member of his in-laws' family and his slave-owning neighbors and friends were fighting for or openly supporting the South.

Buchanan crossed the Potomac River and reached Richmond about September 4. He received a captain's commission, and after heading the Confederate navy's Office of Orders and Detail, he was placed in command of the James River defenses in Virginia. He commanded the ironclad CSS *Virginia* (the *Merrimack*) as she rammed and sank the USS *Cumberland*, shelled the USS *Congress* into submission and watched as the USS *Minnesota* run aground at Hampton Roads on March 8, 1862.

Buchanan struggled to finish off the *Congress*, despite knowing that his brother, McKean Buchanan, was the ship's paymaster. While standing on the *Virginia*'s deck, he was cut down by a bullet that a Federal infantryman had fired from shore. Seriously wounded, Buchanan was relieved of command before the *Virginia*'s history-making battle with the USS *Monitor* the next day.

After recovering from his wound, Buchanan was promoted to admiral in August 1862 and was sent to command Confederate naval forces in Mobile, Alabama. He oversaw construction of the ironclad CSS *Tennessee* and was onboard the ship during her gallant battle with Rear Admiral David Farragut's Federal fleet on August 5, 1864, at the Battle of Mobile Bay. Wounded again and taken prisoner during the battle, Buchanan was not exchanged until February 1865. He was on convalescent leave until the war ended.

Following the war, Buchanan returned to Maryland, where, during 1868–69, he served as president of the Maryland Agricultural College, now the University of Maryland. The college had fewer than a dozen students when Buchanan took over, and it was on the verge of going under. He reduced tuition and enrollment increased to over one hundred. But the tuition reduction landed the school $6,000 in debt—a fact Buchanan neglected to mention to the trustees. He then failed to file the college's annual report, as required by law. The final straw came when Buchanan fired two of the four faculty members without reporting to the trustees, as the college's bylaws required. The trustees sustained one of the firings, but that wasn't good enough for Buchanan. He resigned and moved to Mobile to work for an insurance company. Buchanan returned to Maryland and died at his estate in Talbot County in 1874. He is buried in the Lloyd family plot at Wye House near Easton.

In 1919, the U.S. Navy commissioned the first USS *Buchanan* to honor "Old Buck." A *Wickes*-class destroyer, the *Buchanan* saw action in World War II after being transferred to the Royal Navy. In 1942, as the HMS *Campbeltown*, she was loaded with four tons of explosives and destroyed while ramming the gates of a German dry dock at Saint-Nazaire in occupied France.

On May 11, 1961, almost exactly one hundred years after Buchanan submitted his resignation to Gideon Welles, the U.S. Navy launched a guided missile destroyer, the second USS *Buchanan*. Buchanan's great-granddaughter christened the ship, and hanging below the huge U.S. flag on her bow was a small Confederate battle flag. The band struck up "Maryland, My Maryland," the poem and song inspired by the Pratt Street Riot, which had prompted Buchanan's resignation from the U.S. Navy. The principal speaker on that occasion was Admiral Ulysses S. Grant Sharp.

As Craig L. Symonds puts it in his biography of Buchanan,

> *the irony that assails the modern reader in considering this tableau* [the events of the launching] *suggests the dissonance inherent in the life of a man who devoted himself wholeheartedly to his duty, and yet ended his career fighting against the navy he had so dearly loved.*[5]

RAPHAEL SEMMES

Raphael Semmes was born in Charles County, Maryland, in 1809. He was a descendant of one of the first families to settle Maryland in the 1630s. His mother died when Raphael was very young. His father remarried and moved the family to Washington, D.C. Semmes may have spent a few years at a military academy in St. Mary's County, but he was "essentially self-educated: a lifelong, intent autodidact, never more at home than when lost in a book."[6]

One of his uncles owned a fleet of merchant ships, and after spending some time around the ships and sailors, Semmes decided on a life at sea. In 1826, after a six-year apprenticeship, including time at the naval school at the Norfolk Naval Yard, he formally entered the U.S. Navy as a midshipman. But promotion was slow in the peacetime navy, and there were mandatory extended leaves on shore at reduced pay.

To occupy his time and pick up some extra money, Semmes took a leave of absence in 1831 to read law with his brother in Cumberland, Maryland. He was admitted to the Maryland bar in 1835. Legal work suited his studious habits and his flair for the written language. He would work as a lawyer off and on for the rest of his life.

In 1837, Semmes was finally promoted to lieutenant. He served on routine surveys of the Southern and Gulf coasts and gained a reputation for clashing with his superiors and as a maverick "sea lawyer," a malcontent overly inclined to question and quibble.

In 1833, when a military magazine criticized a favorite teacher at Norfolk, Semmes sent a sharp reply. Thus began a lifelong pattern of firing off polemics to newspapers and magazines.[7] Three years later, when a steamship under his command ran aground and sank in a Florida river, a local newspaper reported that Semmes's action had ruined an upcoming military expedition against the Seminoles. Semmes sent a furious rebuttal, bristling with italics, which the newspaper printed.[8] In 1843, Semmes clashed with his superior officer at the Pensacola Naval Yard and sent a complaint to the Navy Department in Washington.

Semmes commanded the brig USS *Somers* in the early stages of the Mexican War, only to lose his ship and half his crew in a violent storm off Vera Cruz. A court of inquiry acquitted him of any wrongdoing and he went on to serve with distinction for the balance of the war.

While on extended leave after the Mexican War, Semmes practiced law in Mobile, Alabama. He kept asking for sea duty, but he was continuously turned down. His reputation as a quarrelsome subordinate, as well as his languor and bookishness, were the probable reasons. David Dixon Porter wrote,

> *He had no particular taste for his profession, but had a fondness for literature and was a good talker and writer. Although his courage was undoubted, his tastes were rather those of the scholar than of the dashing naval officer.*[9]

Semmes was promoted to commander in 1855. In 1856, he was assigned to lighthouse duties around Mobile, and in 1858 he received a desk job in Washington as secretary to the lighthouse board in the Treasury Department. As the secession crisis worsened in 1860–61, Semmes's family was deeply divided. His brother Samuel, still practicing law in Cumberland, was an ardent pro-Unionist. A cousin, Alexander Semmes, would become a flag officer (commodore) in the U.S. Navy. Raphael's wife Anne, originally from Cincinnati, lined up with her pro-Union Ohio relatives. Their children, mostly raised in Mobile, all supported the Confederacy. Their two eldest boys joined the Confederate army. On February 14, 1861, Alabama's provisional Confederate government summoned Semmes to naval duty. The next day, Semmes resigned from the U.S. Navy. His wife left for Cincinnati with the younger children and lived there for the duration of the war.

Appointed a commander in the Confederate navy in April 1861, Semmes was sent to New Orleans to convert a steamer into the cruiser CSS *Sumter*, the Confederacy's first warship. He ran the *Sumter* through the Federal naval blockade in June 1861 and began a career of commerce raiding that is perhaps unequaled in naval history. During the *Sumter*'s six months of operations in the West Indies and Atlantic, Semmes captured eighteen merchant vessels and skillfully eluded pursuing Federal warships. With his ship badly in need of overhaul, he brought her into Gibraltar in January 1862 and laid her up when the arrival of Federal cruisers made a return to sea impossible.

After Semmes and his officers made their way to England, he was promoted to captain and given command of the British-built cruiser CSS *Alabama*. From August 1862 until June 1864, Semmes took the *Alabama*

Rear Admiral Raphael Semmes, Confederate States Navy, with Confederate flag.
Courtesy of the U.S. Naval Historical Center.

through the Atlantic, into the Gulf of Mexico, around the Cape of Good Hope and into the East Indies, capturing merchantmen and sinking one Federal warship, the USS *Hatteras*. At the end of her long cruise, the *Alabama* was blockaded at Cherbourg, France, while seeking repairs. On June 19, 1864, Semmes took her to sea to fight the Federal cruiser USS *Kearsarge* and was wounded before the *Alabama* was sunk in action. Rescued by a British yacht, Semmes was taken to England, recovered and made his way back to the Confederacy. In little less then two years, the *Alabama*'s crew had sunk or burned sixty-nine merchant vessels.

Semmes became the South's chief naval hero. Partly due to his hero status, Semmes was promoted to rear admiral in February 1865, and he commanded the James River Squadron during the final months of the war. With the fall of Richmond, Semmes was ordered to destroy his ships and join the retreating Confederate army in Danville, Virginia. In Danville, Semmes was assigned the rank of brigadier general and ordered to convert his sailors into an artillery battalion. As a result, Semmes again made history as probably the only American to have worn a star while serving in two separate branches of the military in wartime.

Semmes was to link up with Joseph Johnston's army in North Carolina, but Johnston quickly surrendered to Sherman. Semmes was paroled in Greensboro and made his way back to Mobile. On December 15, a detachment of U.S. Marines arrested Semmes on the somewhat preposterous charge of illegally escaping Federal custody after surrendering the *Alabama* in Cherbourg. He was taken to New York and later confined at the Washington Naval Yard.

Semmes's situation was more political than criminal. He had become something of a symbol of the growing tug of war between President Andrew Johnson, who intended to follow Lincoln's policy of leniency to former Confederates, and an increasingly revanchist Congress. The government intended to put Semmes on trial by military commission, but the Supreme Court had ruled in the meantime that military trials after hostilities had concluded were unconstitutional.[10] In the end, he was held for about four months, but was never put on trial and the charges against him were finally dropped.

Semmes's victories on the *Sumter* and *Alabama*, combined with those of James Iredell Waddell on the CSS *Shenandoah*, John Taylor Wood on the CSS *Tallahassee* and John Newland Maffit on the CSS *Florida*, virtually destroyed the North's merchant fleet and it recovered very slowly in the postwar years. Many Northern merchants and shipping lines "re-flagged" their vessels as foreign ships or sold them outright to Europeans. In 1860, American ships had carried two-thirds of the commerce of New York; by

1863, under the influence of rising insurance rates resulting from the presence of the Confederate raiders, three-fourths was being carried by foreign bottoms. By the close of the war, 715 American vessels had been transferred to British ownership to escape capture or bankruptcy, and another 250 had been sunk or burned.[11] The destruction Semmes had caused as a Confederate naval commander so embittered Northern public opinion that, although he received a pardon with other Southern leaders after the war, his civil liberties were never completely restored.

Following his release Semmes was elected a probate court judge in Mobile, became a professor of philosophy and literature at the Louisiana State Seminary (now Louisiana State University) and a newspaper editor for the *Memphis Daily Bulletin*. He later returned to Mobile and resumed his law practice.

Semmes wrote about his service during the Mexican War and his commands aboard the *Sumter* and *Alabama*. His *Memoirs of Service Afloat* (1868) is a summary of his Confederate naval career and an excellent exemplar of the theory of the "Lost Cause."

Despite his ill treatment after the war, many of his former colleagues in the U.S. Navy became grudging admirers. Contrasting his poor reputation before the war with the energy he showed onboard the *Sumter* and *Alabama*, David Dixon Porter, himself one of the frustrated commanders who had pursued Semmes, wrote:

> *He was indolent and fond of his comfort, so that altogether his associates in the Navy gave him credit for very little energy. What was, then, the astonishment of his old companions to find that Semmes was pursuing a course that required the greatest skill and vigor; for there never was a naval commander who in so short a time committed such depredations on an enemy's commerce, or who so successfully eluded the vessels sent in pursuit of him…The inertness he had displayed while in the United States Navy had disappeared…He had become a new man.*[12]

Semmes died in Mobile in 1877 and is buried there. Like Buchanan, U.S. naval vessels have borne his name. The first USS *Semmes* was a *Clemson*-class destroyer that saw action in World War II and also served as a Coast Guard vessel. The second USS *Semmes* was an *Adams*-class guided missile destroyer. It was struck from the navy list in 1991 and sold to Greece. And some "Trekkies" have apparently divined that the third USS *Semmes* will be a *Larson*-class Federation starship in the twenty-third century![13]

RICHARD THOMAS ZARVONA

The use of disguises for spying and raiding expeditions during the Civil War is an often overlooked subject. There are several verified instances of soldiers and irregulars disguised as women on both sides of the conflict. Perhaps the most unusual cross-dressing episode of the war involved a Marylander, the Confederate officer known as Richard Thomas Zarvona.[1]

Richard Thomas Jr. (his birth name) came from a notable St. Mary's County family. His father had been Speaker of the Maryland House of Delegates and president of the Senate. An uncle had been governor. The Thomas estate, Mattapany, had once been the residence of Charles Calvert, the third Lord Baltimore and Lord Proprietor of Maryland. (Mattapany is now the commander's official residence at the Patuxent Naval Air Station.)

Thomas seems to have been born for adventure. At age sixteen, he entered West Point, but his preference for the "martial arts" instead of the civil engineering courses that dominated the curriculum at that time led to his standing near the bottom of the first-year class. He resigned early in his second year.

Family legend has it that Thomas then worked on government surveys in California and other points in the West. He made his way to China, where he helped to protect coastal shipping from pirates. He later turned up in Italy and observed or participated in Giuseppe Garibaldi's revolutionary struggle for Italian unification and independence.

Thomas reportedly also spent time in France, where he learned to speak the language fluently and, according to family lore, fell in love with a French girl, who drowned. He felt her loss so deeply that he took her name and thereafter chose to be known as Richard Thomas Zarvona.

Evidence also suggests that sometime during his stay in Europe Zarvona spent time with the French Zouaves. The Zouaves (pronounced zoo-AHVES) derived their name from the Zouaoua, a tribe of Berbers from the Algerian mountains. Zouave regiments were first formed in 1831 and soon became a regular part of the French army. The Zouaves gained a reputation for their strict discipline and fighting ability, but more famously for their unusual uniforms, consisting of red, flared-out pantaloons, blue doublets, crimson fezzes, white gaiters and scimitar-like sabers.

The Zouave uniform became very popular in the United States in the pre–Civil War years and many voluntary militia units fitted themselves out as Zouaves. Several Zouave regiments were in the field during the war. The Union army had Zouave regiments throughout the war, while the Confederates fielded only a handful of units.

Zarvona returned to Maryland shortly before hostilities broke out in April 1861. His two younger brothers had already gone south to enlist in the Confederate army, and Zarvona was expected to stay home to take care of their mother. But given his prior exploits, it would have been impossible for him to stay out of the fight. He crossed the Potomac, and in May he formed the nucleus of what he hoped would be a Confederate Zouave regiment on the Virginia side of the Potomac. In Richmond, Zarvona met Virginia Governor John Letcher, who introduced him to George N. Hollins.

A Baltimorean and a forty-six-year veteran of the U.S. Navy, Hollins had been appointed a captain in the Confederate navy. He later became one of the Confederate navy's few "flag officers" (commodores). Crossing the Potomac en route to Richmond, Hollins had observed the *St. Nicholas*, a steamer that carried passengers between Baltimore, Point Lookout and ports along the Potomac. The *St. Nicholas* also served as the supply ship for the USS *Pawnee*, a Federal gunboat that was part of the Potomac Flotilla, a small fleet organized to protect travel and supplies to Washington as well as to interdict people and goods flowing from Confederate sympathizers in Southern Maryland across the river into Virginia.

The *Pawnee* was much feared in Virginia. There were wild rumors floating about that she had been ordered to steam into the James River and attack the Confederate capital, which early in the war was virtually defenseless from the water. Richmond had been momentarily thrown into a panic.[2]

Zarvona and Hollins formulated a plan for seizing both the *St. Nicholas* and the *Pawnee*. Letcher at first viewed Zarvona as an eccentric, but he changed his mind after Zarvona presented the details of the plan. Zarvona proposed going to Baltimore with some of his Zouaves to enlist help from a dozen or more Southern sympathizers. They would board the *St. Nicholas* as passengers, and at the right moment on the Potomac and

Confederate soldier in Zouave uniform. *Courtesy of the Maryland State Archives.*

Gunboat USS *Pawnee*. *Courtesy of the U.S. Naval Historical Center.*

at a given signal, Hollins would seize the vessel, steer her into the Coan River on the Virginia side and gather up Confederate reinforcements before steaming alongside the *Pawnee* to capture the Federal ship.

Letcher requested that the Confederate secretary of the navy supply arms and ammunition for the expedition. He gave Hollins a draft for $1,000 to procure weapons and pay inducements to volunteers who would join the enterprise. Letcher promised Zarvona a colonelcy if the plan succeeded and told him he could use the title when enlisting recruits. Hollins signed the draft over to Zarvona, who along with a comrade—George W. Alexander, a former U.S. Navy engineer— furtively made his way to Baltimore.

His recruiting efforts were successful. On the evening of June 28, 1861, Zarvona's men boarded the *St. Nicholas* in Baltimore. They arrived at the wharf one by one and in pairs so as not to arouse suspicion. They were searched for contraband, as military authorities required, but nothing was found.

Among the nearly sixty passengers boarding the steamer was a stylishly dressed young lady, who spoke broken English with a strong French accent. Her brother, a fierce-looking bearded man, traveled with her as her translator. Her name was Madame LaForte, she said, and she had a number of large trunks with her because she wanted to set up a millinery business in Washington. Entranced by her smile, the purser assigned her a large stateroom off the main deck and had deckhands haul her trunks to the cabin.

When the *St. Nicholas* departed, the lady emerged from her stateroom and began to flirt shamelessly with the male passengers and ship's officers. The captain, who prided himself on his knowledge of French, tried out his skills on the lady, who indeed appeared to be a native of France with a stream of coquettish language that quite overwhelmed him. She covered her eyes and cheeks with a veil. She tossed her fan about and cocked her head at an angle toward any gentleman who occupied her attention. With her brother on her arm, she wandered about the steamer, flirting as she went.

For some reason the crew didn't understand, many of the passengers elected to wander around the decks well into the night as the *St. Nicholas* made her way South. About midnight, as the steamer rounded Point Lookout into the Potomac, she put into a wharf and took on several more male passengers. The passengers, it later turned out, were Hollins and other members of the Confederate navy.

George Watts, one of Zarvona's recruits, was worried. Wandering about the decks, he hadn't seen anyone resembling Zarvona. Had the colonel missed the boat, as it were? He felt sure he would be arrested as a Rebel spy, sent to Fort McHenry and hanged.

Just then, George W. Alexander, the "French lady's" bearded brother, tapped him on the shoulder and said he was wanted in a nearby cabin. As Watts explained in an interview in the *Baltimore Evening Sun* in 1910,

> *I hurried to the cabin and found all our boys gathered around that frisky French lady. She looked at me when I came in, and Lord, I knew those eyes! It was the Colonel. The French lady then shed her bonnet, wig and dress and stepped forth clad in a brilliant new Zouave uniform. In a jiffy the "French lady's" three trunks were dragged out and opened. One was filled with cutlasses, another with Colt revolvers and the third with carbines. Each man buckled on a sword and pistol and grabbed a gun, and then the Colonel told us what to do.*

Zarvona and Hollins confronted the boat's captain, who, when told that thirty armed men were aboard, quickly surrendered command. The Confederates who had boarded in Baltimore and Hollins's men, who had come aboard at Point Lookout, seized the steamer, and the Confederate naval crew steered her toward the Coan River on the Virginia side of the Potomac.

In the early morning hours of June 29, the *St. Nicholas* docked in the Coan River in Northumberland County and took aboard thirty Confederate soldiers. The passengers were permitted to leave with their possessions.

Then came disappointing news. Confederate sharpshooters had killed the *Pawnee*'s captain and the gunboat had returned to the Washington Naval

Yard for the funeral. It would be impossible to wait for her return, so what could they do?

Bent on making the *St. Nicholas*'s seizure worthwhile, Hollins ordered the steamer to head into the Chesapeake for a raiding expedition that would compensate for the lost opportunity with the *Pawnee*.

The *Monticello*, a brig heading to Baltimore from Brazil and laden with thirty-five thousand bags of coffee, became their first prize. Confederate sailors took her over and sailed her to Fredericksburg, where coffee was in short supply. Their next victim was the *Mary Pierce*, ten days out of Boston and bound for Washington with a load of ice. A prize crew took her to Fredericksburg also, where the local hospitals welcomed the ice.

The *St. Nicholas* was running desperately short of coal. Luckily, the schooner *Margaret* soon hove into view, bound from Alexandria to New York with a cargo of coal. By this time, Zarvona and Hollins were worried that the seizure of the *St. Nicholas* had been discovered and feared that Yankee ships would be looking for her. Hollins ordered the *St. Nicholas*, with the *Margaret* in tow, to set a course for the Rappahannock and Fredericksburg. The Confederates received an enthusiastic welcome in Fredericksburg. A ball was given in their honor, and Zarvona delighted those present by appearing in the hoops and skirts of the lady milliner from France.

Zarvona was honored and entertained in Richmond as well. He had played an invaluable role in achieving the Confederate navy's first victory. On the Fourth of July, Zarvona and his Zouave troops paraded through the city streets, to much acclaim.

But Zarvona's success quickly led to his downfall. Growing restless in Richmond, he began planning his next raid. He resolved to repeat his triumph by seizing another steamer out of Baltimore.

Soon, Federal intelligence agents learned from spies on both sides of the Potomac that a small boat had come over from the Coan River to Maryland and had landed the crews from the *St. Nicholas* and the other captured vessels. The boat was said to be heading up the bay. She was manned by well-armed men, variously estimated from eighteen to thirty in number. By July 8, 1861, these men had abandoned their boat and had taken passage on the steamer *Mary Washington*, headed for Baltimore.

Unfortunately for Zarvona and his comrades, who should be onboard the *Mary Washington* but the crews of the *St. Nicholas* and the other ships they had captured and just returned to Maryland. Things got even dicier when some Federal soldiers and police officers boarded at Fairhaven, a resort south of Annapolis.

Zarvona's former prisoners quickly tipped off the soldiers. He and his comrades were kept under observation but were not arrested to avoid a

Caricature of Richard Thomas Zarvona as the "French Lady." *Courtesy of artist David Clark.*

possible armed confrontation. But as the steamer neared Baltimore, Zarvona grew worried that he had been identified. He tried to lower a lifeboat to escape but was stopped by some officers. Zarvona drew a pistol and the officers drew their revolvers. The officers informed Zarvona that they would take him dead or alive. He called out for "his boys" to help, and by that means the Federals discovered who the rest of the Rebels were onboard.

In the meantime, the Federal commander had ordered the *Mary Washington*'s captain to steer for Fort McHenry so troops could be brought aboard to seize the Rebels. When it became common knowledge that the steamer was heading for the fort, the passengers raised a commotion, some trying to aid the Confederates while others sided with the Federals. When the *Mary Washington* docked at Fort McHenry, a detachment of infantry went onboard and marched Zarvona's accomplices off to confinement.

But somehow during the commotion, the Colonel had slipped away. Some female Confederate sympathizers had stuffed him into a bureau in the ladies' cabin. Removing the bottoms of the drawers, they had fitted the slender Zarvona into place. He was finally located after an hour and a half of searching. Some reports say he was once again dressed as a woman when he was found. The "French spy lady," as he was being called in both the North and the South, was a sad spectacle as he was dragged, cramped and drenched with perspiration, off to prison.

Zarvona was placed in solitary confinement in Fort McHenry. In his baggage were found his Zouave uniform, some letters confirming his mission of depredation on Chesapeake shipping, his commission in the volunteer forces of Virginia and a letter of credit drawn on a Baltimore bank. These were all used as evidence against him.

Northern military authorities charged Zarvona with piracy and treason, and ignored repeated requests that he be exchanged. In December 1861, Zarvona was transferred to Fort Lafayette in New York Harbor.

Zarvona remained in solitary confinement at Fort Lafayette, his every move under close observation. His correspondence was intercepted and read. His health rapidly deteriorated. His mother's efforts to visit him were rebuffed.

Aroused by reports reaching him about Zarvona's condition and treatment, in January 1863 Governor Letcher wrote a letter to President Lincoln. In it, he protested the Federal military's failure to treat Zarvona as a prisoner of war even though he was carrying a military commission when captured. He also complained that the colonel had by that time been held for eighteen months without a trial. Letcher stated that he would place some Federal prisoners of war in solitary confinement in Virginia prisons in retaliation for Zarvona's treatment. They would remain there until Zarvona was properly exchanged and returned to Virginia.

The governor was as good as his word. By February, the seven Federal soldiers Letcher had transferred to solitary confinement were writing letters to the War Department in Washington, pleading for Zarvona's release. Wives, relatives and friends of the "hostages" mounted an incessant letter-writing campaign to get the U.S. government to relent.

By mid-March, Secretary of War Stanton had concluded that Zarvona's confinement served no further purpose other than to invite additional reprisals from Virginia. On April 11, 1863, the U.S. Army commissioner general of prisoners notified authorities at Fort Delaware (where Zarvona had been transferred) that Stanton had authorized his exchange.

Zarvona reached Richmond on May 6, 1863, his nervous system completely broken down. He immediately proposed that he be given command of the combined Maryland Confederate regiments even though he was obviously unfit for duty and such an assignment would have violated the terms of his parole.

Deeply disappointed, Zarvona sailed for France. He returned to Maryland in 1870, but left for France again, trying to restore the family fortune— he failed. He returned for good in 1872, a shattered man. In 1873, he wrote a rather disconnected account of his life and lived his last years in anguish over his health and declining finances. He felt that his friends had abandoned him and his gallantry had been forgotten. Richard Thomas Zarvona died on March 17, 1875, and was buried at a family estate in St. Mary's County, Maryland.

But Zarvona was not forgotten. Company H of the Forty-seventh Virginia Infantry (Walter's Company) was more commonly called Zarvona's Zouaves during and after the war. A Maryland chapter of the United Daughters of the Confederacy is named for him. In 1990, the Maryland division of the Sons of Confederate Veterans dedicated a marker for his unmarked grave. And perhaps Richard Thomas Zarvona would have taken some consolation from the fact that he and his alter ego, the "French lady," are mentioned over seventy times in the *Official Records of the War of the Rebellion*.

HUNTER DAVIDSON, JAMES IREDELL WADDELL AND MARYLAND'S OYSTER NAVY

Two naval officers share the rare distinction of being the only documented commanders to have served in three navies, all operating within the borders of the United States. Both began their careers in the U.S. Navy, joined the Confederate navy and became commanders of Maryland's almost-forgotten Oyster Navy. Hunter Davidson and James Iredell Waddell led parallel lives in many respects.

Hunter Davidson

Davidson was born in the District of Columbia in 1827, and in 1841 he became a student at the Naval School of Virginia, one of the precursors of the U.S. Naval Academy. He transferred to the newly created naval academy and graduated in 1847. In 1855, he attained the rank of lieutenant.

In April 1861, Davidson joined the Confederate navy and briefly served at the Norfolk Naval Yard and onboard the CSS *Patrick Henry*. From March to May 1862, he was a lieutenant on the ironclad CSS *Virginia* (the *Merrimack*) during her brief but celebrated history.

Davidson became an expert at designing and laying "torpedoes," the contemporary term for naval mines. Davidson's interest in undertaking this type of work might have come from a Confederate naval directive rewarding the inventor of a device that destroyed an enemy vessel with 50 percent of the value of the vessel and its armament. He became commander of the gunboat CSS *Teaser* and was in charge of the submarine battery that mined the James River. On April 9, 1964, while commanding the torpedo boat CSS *Squib*, Davidson sailed past the Federal fleet at Newport News, attacked the USS *Minnesota* with a spar torpedo and escaped back up the James.

Coincidentally (or perhaps not), the *Minnesota* was one of the ships the *Virginia* had planned to attack during its first day of combat on March 8, 1862, but darkness had prevented it. The *Virginia* (on which Davidson served) was bearing down on the *Minnesota* on the ninth, and only the timely intervention of the USS *Monitor* prevented the *Virginia* from finishing off the *Minnesota*. The *Squib*'s assault on the *Minnesota* apparently did little damage, since she continued in service until the war's end as the flagship of the North Atlantic Blockading Squadron.

Davidson's bold action on the *Squib* resulted in his being promoted to commander. His final Civil War service took him to Europe, where he was made commander of the CSS *City of Richmond*. The *City of Richmond*'s original mission was to take on supplies for building naval mines, but she was soon assigned to escort and act as a supply ship to the ironclad ram CSS *Stonewall*.

The *Stonewall* had been built in France for the Confederate navy, but the French government embargoed the ship in February 1864 and subsequently sold her to Denmark. Upon her completion in late 1864, the Danish government would not accept delivery, and her builder secretly resold her to the Confederates.

Commissioned at sea, the *Stonewall* headed for the Azores en route to America. Forced into Ferrol, Spain, by a storm, she was confronted by two U.S. warships in March 1865, but the Federal vessels refused to engage the heavily armed Confederate ironclad. After calling at Lisbon, the *Stonewall* crossed the Atlantic and reached Havana in May. Since the war by that time had ended, the *Stonewall*'s captain turned her over to Spanish authorities. Davidson surrendered his ship at Nassau.

In the first episode of what was to become a lengthy involvement with Latin America, in 1866 Davidson turned up in Valparaiso, Chile, with a ship carrying arms and torpedoes. The purpose of the expedition isn't known, but it seems that his ship arrived too late to complete whatever transaction had been intended and the venture was a financial failure. There is some evidence that the artist James McNeill Whistler may have arranged the sale or distribution of the weapons. Whistler appeared in Valparaiso at the same time, and he and Davidson were apparently friends.

JAMES IREDELL WADDELL

Much has been written about James Iredell Waddell's Confederate naval career. Born in Pittsboro, North Carolina, in 1824, he became a midshipman in the U.S. Navy in 1841 and spent nearly twenty years onboard ships, saw action during the Mexican War and was an instructor

Commander Hunter Davidson, Confederate States Navy. *Courtesy of the U.S. Naval Historical Center.*

at the naval academy shortly before the outbreak of the Civil War. While in Annapolis, Waddell married Anne Sellman Iglehart, the daughter of a prominent local merchant.

Waddell's sympathies lay with the South. He secretly entered the service of the Confederacy in Baltimore. He resigned his commission and his name was struck from the U.S. Navy rolls in January 1862. He received a commission as lieutenant in the Confederate navy on May 27, 1862. He was briefly assigned to an ironclad on the Mississippi, but due to the scarcity of ships in the Confederate navy, he was transferred to commanding shore batteries. His battery participated in the repulse of the Federal flotilla during the Battle of Drewry's Bluff in May 1862 on the James River, and he later performed similar service in defense of Charleston, South Carolina, until March 1863.

In March 1863, Waddell was sent to England to await a seagoing assignment. His opportunity finally arrived in October 1864, when he assumed command of the British-built steamer *Sea King* and converted her to the Confederate cruiser CSS *Shenandoah* off the Madeira Islands. Waddell took the *Shenandoah* through the South Atlantic and into the Indian Ocean, capturing several U.S. merchant vessels along the way. Sailing into the North Pacific and Bering Sea, Waddell captured and destroyed nearly three-dozen merchantmen and whalers between April and July 1865.

Some of the captured ships had newspapers reporting that Richmond had fallen and the Confederate government was retreating to Danville, Virginia, but Waddell dismissed such reports as Yankee propaganda. Moreover, he reasonably concluded that if the Confederacy hadn't actually surrendered, there was still a government to fight for. But on August 2, 1865, just as the *Shenandoah* was about to sail off to shell San Francisco, Waddell received irrefutable confirmation that the Confederacy was no more. The *Shenandoah* came upon a British merchantman, whose captain informed Waddell that the Confederacy had collapsed. Consequently, the *Shenandoah* was no longer a man-of-war but a pirate ship without a country, liable to seizure under international law.

Fearing that he and his crew would be tried as pirates for their post-surrender "depredations," Waddell decided on a unique plan. Instead of returning to the United States and surrendering there, Waddell dismounted his guns and charted a course that would take the *Shenandoah* around Cape Horn and up the Atlantic to England. He surrendered his ship and command in Liverpool on November 2, 1865, hauling down the last Confederate flag still in active service. The *Shenandoah* entered history as the only Confederate warship to have circumnavigated the globe.

MARYLAND'S OYSTER NAVY

The history and origin of Maryland's Oyster Navy (sometimes called the Maryland State Flotilla) have been almost forgotten. Before the Civil War, Maryland had enacted legislation to conserve the supply of oysters in Chesapeake Bay by regulating the methods of taking them and outlawing the transport of oysters out of the state in boats not owned by Marylanders. However, enforcement was left to the county sheriffs, and results were meager.

By the 1860s, with the arrival of the railroads, commercial shucking houses, canneries and the use of oyster shells as fertilizer, the oyster industry had become a major business. In 1865, the Maryland General Assembly enacted comprehensive legislation regulating the taking of oysters. But major problems in policing the law—such as keeping boats from other states off Maryland oyster beds, keeping dredgers out of areas limited to tonging, arresting unlicensed vessels, assuring that dredgers only used sails and preventing oyster catching out of season—remained.

Enter the Oyster Navy. In 1867, the General Assembly authorized chartering a steamer to patrol the bay and apprehend oyster law violators. In 1868, at the prodding of the oyster industry, the state established the board of commissioners of the State Oyster Police Force. The steamer *Leila* was built in Baltimore in 1869 and was the flagship of the nascent "navy." Other steamers and sloops were added over the years.[1]

Hunter Davidson became the first commander of the Oyster Navy. He commanded the flagship *Leila* (which he named after his daughter) and equipped her with ordnance taken from a former Confederate vessel. He prepared the initial internal rules and regulations and the shipping articles that each officer and crewman had to sign upon joining.[2] Davidson served until 1872. Later that year, he moved to Argentina, having accepted an invitation from Thomas Jefferson Page, the CSS *Stonewall*'s former commander. He advised the Argentine navy on the purchase of mines and torpedo boats. In 1874, he was appointed commander of the Argentine navy's torpedo boat squadron. He led a scientific expedition up the Paraguay River and continued rendering services to the Argentine navy until he resigned in 1885. He died in Paraguay in 1913.

Still worried about piracy charges, Waddell remained in England until 1875, when Confederate veterans received a general amnesty. That year, he returned to Annapolis and took a job as captain on Pacific Mail Line Company vessels. As captain of the steamer *City of San Francisco*, Waddell sailed the South Pacific, close to the waters where ten years before he had caused considerable devastation. Calling at Honolulu in 1876, the arrival of

Commander James Iredell Waddell, Confederate States Navy. *Courtesy of the U.S. Naval Historical Center.*

The James Iredell Waddell house in Annapolis.

the dreaded *Shenandoah*'s skipper apparently went unnoticed. But as his ship left port the next day, the Royal Hawaiian Band struck up "Dixie." Waddell, being a true Southern gentleman, dipped his flag in salute.

Back in Annapolis in 1883, Waddell was appointed captain of the new Oyster Navy steamer *Governor Hamilton* and was given a seat on the Oyster Commission. He wrote the part of the commission's report recommending the addition of more steamers and the appointment of commanders on merit rather than through political connections. In 1884, Waddell was named commander of the Oyster Navy.

By the early 1880s, the Oyster Navy was in trouble. It suffered from lack of funds, had become a source of patronage and was ineffective at curbing illegal oyster dredging. Waddell's principal task was to step up enforcement. Two weeks after his appointment as commander, Waddell ran the *Leila* into the midst of a fleet of illegal dredgers at the mouth of the Honga River in Dorchester County. The oystermen didn't take this attempt to enforce the oyster laws seriously, which was a big mistake. Waddell ordered the *Leila*'s crew to open fire. Within fifteen minutes, they had sunk one boat, run three ashore, captured another three and put the rest to flight.

Waddell was well on his way to eradicating the Chesapeake's "oyster pirates" as head of the State Fisheries Force (by then the official name of the Oyster Navy) when he died on March 16, 1886. His pallbearers and escort were former Confederate naval and army officers. He is buried in St. Anne's Cemetery in Annapolis, and his imposing brick Victorian house stands at 61 College Avenue across from St. John's College.

Local legend has it that Waddell built his imposing home with the prize money he received from the ships he had captured on the *Shenandoah*. This is unlikely, however, since Waddell sank or burned the ships he captured. Moreover, the *Shenandoah* didn't carry extra crewmen to sail the vessels to prize courts, and prize courts in neutral countries were not open to Confederate warships. The Annapolis chapter of the Sons of Confederate Veterans bears his name. The USS *Waddell*, an *Adams*-class guided missile destroyer, was commissioned in 1964. It saw action during the Vietnam War, was decommissioned in 1992 and was sold to Greece.

Maryland's Oyster Navy (today the Natural Resources Police Force) survives and is the state's oldest law enforcement agency, as well as one of the oldest conservation law enforcement agencies in the country. Its creation, growth and successes would not have been possible without the efforts of the two Civil War naval veterans who brought it to life and became the state of Maryland's most notable "naval" commanders.

BASIL LANNEAU GILDERSLEEVE, CONFEDERATE SCHOLAR-SOLDIER

ivil War buffs are certainly familiar with the life and career of Joshua Lawrence Chamberlain, the Bowdoin College professor who left the halls of academe to answer the Union's call and became the "Hero of Little Round Top" at Gettysburg. But few today recall the name of Basil Lanneau Gildersleeve, a Confederate scholar-soldier who served honorably, if somewhat eccentrically, in the Army of Northern Virginia and whose wartime experiences left a permanent mark on his literary work.

By any estimation, Gildersleeve was one of the greatest classical scholars the United States has ever produced. He was born in Charleston, South Carolina, in 1831, the son of a Presbyterian minister who never held a pulpit but instead owned and edited religious newspapers. Showing an early talent for learning and languages, Gildersleeve wrote that he had read the Bible from cover to cover when he was five, learned enough Latin to get through Caesar, Cicero, Virgil and Horace and enough Greek to "make out" the New Testament before he was thirteen.[1] He had a distinctively literary bent, writing essays and reviews and trying a novel in his early twenties.

After first studying at the College of Charleston and Pennsylvania's Jefferson College, Gildersleeve entered the College of New Jersey (now Princeton University) as a junior and graduated fourth in his class in 1849. One of his classmates was Maryland Confederate general Bradley T. Johnson. He studied classical philology in Germany and earned a PhD from the University of Göttingen in 1853. Just before his twenty-fifth birthday, he began a twenty-year career as a professor at the University of Virginia, where he taught Greek and Latin.

Considering himself "a Charlestonian first, Carolinian next, and then a Southerner,"[2] there was no doubt where Gildersleeve's sympathies lay when hostilities broke out in 1861. He joined the Confederate army but, unlike

Professor Basil Lanneau Gildersleeve of the Johns Hopkins University. *Courtesy of the Maryland Historical Society.*

Chamberlain, he did not take a leave of absence from his teaching duties. The University of Virginia, unlike most Southern colleges, did not close its doors during the war. It struggled on with a student body composed of the maimed, the wounded and boys too young for military service.

Gildersleeve "soldiered" on summer vacations from the university. During successive summers, he served on the staff of the Twenty-first Virginia Infantry and was a private in the First Virginia Cavalry. The summer of 1864 saw him on the staff of General John B. Gordon. While carrying orders for Gordon, he was wounded when a bullet from a Spencer rifle broke his thighbone and his leg was nearly amputated. Of that experience, Gildersleeve later wrote,

> *I lost my pocket Homer, I lost my pistol, I lost one of my horses, and finally I came very near to losing my life from a wound which kept me five months on my back.*[3]

Gildersleeve convalesced at the home of General Raleigh Colston, whose eldest daughter, Elizabeth, nursed him and married him two years later. The prospect of a defeated South dominated by the North prompted him to consider immigrating to Mexico. Instead, he returned to the University of Virginia and helped rebuild it. On returning to teaching, he became something of an institution at UVA, with his cutaway coat and silk hat, his full black beard and the limp from his war wound. His erudition and biting wit made him a popular, though demanding, teacher.[4]

On one occasion, he was able to help a fellow academic prodigy. In 1868, a sixteen-year-old UVA student petitioned to be awarded a bachelor's degree after attending classes for only one year. He claimed his family was too poor to continue to support his studies. The panel appointed to review his petition was impressed with his outstanding record, but refused to grant him a degree. They had granted him a waiver to enter the university when he was fifteen; why should they grant him a waiver to graduate at sixteen?

Undeterred, the student countered that if he couldn't receive the BA, would the university award him an MD degree the next year if he could pass the medical course examinations within that time? This had rarely been done before, and the professors thought that the student was taking on too much. Gildersleeve was on the panel. He had taught the student Greek and knew he was brilliant. He urged his colleagues to give the boy a chance. The professors reluctantly agreed, and the next year Dr. Walter Reed received his medical degree.[5]

Gildersleeve was one of the first professors appointed when the Johns Hopkins University opened its doors in 1876, and his remaining years were spent in Baltimore. A chance to be part of the first German-style research university in the United States was too good an opportunity to pass up. "I certainly did not dream," he wrote, "that so much enthusiasm was left in me."[6] In 1880, he founded the *American Journal of Philology* and edited it for forty years. In addition to his teaching and editorial duties, Gildersleeve produced dozens of critical essays and scholarly articles, as well as an influential study of the Greek poet Pindar, *Syntax of Classical Greek* and *Gildersleeve's Latin Grammar*, which is still in print. In 1891, Gildersleeve praised the richness of the academic climate at Hopkins.

> *The greater freedom of action…the wider and richer life, the opportunities to travel…have stimulated production and have made the last fourteen years my most fruitful years in the eyes of the scholarly world.*[7]

Gildersleeve's Civil War experiences had left an indelible impression. Both of his Princeton roommates, Virginians James Kendall Lee and Peyton Randolph Harrison, were killed at First Bull Run (Manassas). He only reconciled with his alma mater—which, despite a large number of Southern students, had remained strong for the Union—when Princeton awarded him an honorary degree in 1899.

No doubt influenced by the example of his newspaper publisher father, Gildersleeve wrote a series of editorials for the *Richmond Examiner* in 1863–64. Although the editorials appeared after Gettysburg and the fall of Vicksburg, his journalism inveighed more against the "homefront" than the military forces in the field. He criticized the selfishness of speculators, blockade-runners and farmers for profiteering, hoarding and inflicting hardships on soldiers and civilians alike. He was especially harsh on the political leadership, claiming that the main strength of the Confederacy was its people, while the main "awkwardness" was its government.

But Gildersleeve's most incisive writing about the war came during his years in Baltimore. Gildersleeve wrote to the editor of the *Atlantic* in 1891 that

> [e]*ven the most charitable of my Northern friends find it difficult to understand how a Southerner could have gone into the conflict with a clean conscience and whenever a reference is made to the war there is a certain reticence among wellbred people as if the Southern interlocutor had fallen into some heinous sin.*[8]

In 1892, he authored an article entitled "The Creed of the Old South," which appeared in the *Atlantic*. Part personal memoir and smattered with mordent humor and classical references, the article is one of the principal summaries of what became known as the theory of the "Lost Cause."

Gone was the bitterness of the war editorials. Instead, Gildersleeve presented the ideals that impelled the Southern people to war:

> *There is such a thing as fighting for a principle, an idea, but principle and idea must be incarnate, and the principle of States' rights was incarnate in the historical life of the Southern people. Submission to any encroachment on the rights of a State means slavery. To us, submission meant slavery, as it did to Pericles and the Athenians.*[9]

Gildersleeve apparently didn't know, or chose to ignore, Dr. Samuel Johnson's famous statement (speaking of the American colonies during the Revolution), "How is it that we hear the loudest yelps for liberty among the drivers of negroes?"[10] In any event, Gildersleeve did not skirt the issue of slavery. He wrote that

> *we were born to this social order, we had to do our duty in it according to our lights, and this duty was made infinitely more difficult by the*

Gilman Hall at the Johns Hopkins University, where Basil L. Gildersleeve taught and had his office.

interference of those who, as we thought, could not understand the conditions of the problem, and who did not have to bear the expense of the experiments they proposed.[11]

Fighting the war, and defending the war, was about honor, as the Greeks and Romans understood it.

That the cause we fought for and our brothers died for was the cause of civil liberty, and not the cause of human slavery, is a thesis which we feel ourselves bound to maintain whenever our motives are challenged or misunderstood, if only for our children's sake.[12]

The article was a major success and was later reprinted as a book. Its popularity inspired Gildersleeve to publish another article in the *Atlantic* in 1897, entitled "A Southerner in the Peloponnesian War," in which he compared the Civil War to the ancient conflict between the Athenians and Spartans. That work was also printed in book form with his previous essay.
He wrote,

From the night when word was brought that the Federals had occupied Alexandria to the time I hobbled into the provost marshal's office at Charlottesville and took the oath of allegiance, the war was part of my life, and it is not altogether surprising that the memories of the Confederacy come back to me whenever I contemplate the history of the Peloponnesian War.

The Peloponnesian war, like our war, was a war between two leagues, a Northern Union and a Southern Confederacy. The Northern Union, represented by Athens, was a naval power. The Southern Confederacy, under the leadership of Sparta, was a land power. The Athenians represented the progressive element, the Spartans the conservative. The Athenians believed in a strong centralized government. The Lacedaemonians [Spartans] professed greater regard for autonomy… In fact, it would be possible to write the story of our Peloponnesian war in phrases of Thucydides.[13]

Both wars stemmed from sectional conflicts.

There were jealousies enough between Athens and Sparta in the olden times, which correspond to our colonial days…We accept the hostility of Attica and Boeotia, of Attica and Megara; and there are no more graphic chapters than those that set forth the enmity between New York and Maryland, between New Amsterdam and Connecticut.[14]

Slavery, he believed, was not essentially a moral issue.

> *True, there was no slavery question in the Peloponnesian war, for antique civilization without slavery is hardly thinkable; but after all, the slavery question belongs ultimately to the sphere of economics.*[15]

Returning to his favorite theme, literature, he said,

> *The war was a good time for the study of the conflict between Athens and Sparta. It was a good time for reading and re-reading classical literature generally, for the South was blockaded against new books as effectively, almost, as Megara was blockaded against garlic and salt... The Southerner, always conservative in his tastes and no great admirer of American literature, which had become largely alien to him, went back to his English classics, his ancient classics. Old gentlemen past the military age furbished up their Latin and Greek. Some of them had never let their Latin and Greek grow rusty.*[16]

Gildersleeve Hall at Johns Hopkins University.

Although most historians would probably consider Gildersleeve's parallels between the two wars forced and overly simplistic, his portrayal of the effects of the war on the civilian population in the South is compelling. His only oversight, in my opinion, was a failure to evaluate the war through the prism of two concepts the Greeks had much to teach us about: Tragedy and Fate.

Gildersleeve received a number of honorary degrees, and in 1908 he was elected a member of the American Academy of Arts and Letters. His name was included in the major literary histories of his time. In 1912, the National Institute of Arts and Letters compiled a list of the country's "Forty Immortals," and placed Gildersleeve among them, along with Theodore Roosevelt, Henry James, John Muir, John Singer Sargent and Woodrow Wilson. A profile of Gildersleeve that appeared in the *New York Times* in 1923 called him "St. Basil of Baltimore."

Gildersleeve lived to be ninety-two, and he was likely the last person still alive to have known Edgar Allan Poe personally. They both had lived in Richmond in the 1840s, and Gildersleeve, though only a teenager, was a fellow contributor with Poe to the *Southern Literary Messenger*. Gildersleeve liked to recall how he once heard Poe recite his poem, "The Raven."[17]

Gildersleeve retained his lively mind and acerbic wit until the end. Although he supposedly had mellowed over the years, on the eve of his ninety-second birthday, a young reporter from the *Baltimore News* made a bumbling attempt to interview him. No doubt recalling his father and his own journalistic efforts, Gildersleeve said to the hapless reporter, "How long have you been interviewing? You're not particularly good at it."[18]

Gildersleeve died on January 9, 1924, in Baltimore and was buried in the University of Virginia's cemetery in Charlottesville. His headstone contains a quotation from Aeschylus in Greek that is fitting for a scholar-soldier: "Life's bivouac is over."

Gildersleeve's many years in Baltimore are memorialized at Johns Hopkins. The Department of Classics named a professorship in his honor, and Gildersleeve Hall is an undergraduate residence on the Homewood campus.

ANNA ELLA CARROLL

Lincoln's Lady Strategist," the "Great Unrecognized Member of Lincoln's Cabinet," the "Originator of the Tennessee Campaign," the "Woman Who Saved the Union"—all these epithets have been applied to Anna Ella Carroll. An enormous legend has been created around her, a legend she did much to foster.

Was she really the "brains" behind the North's political and military strategy during the war? The evidence is inconclusive, but Carroll deservedly remains a feminist icon.

Anna Ella Carroll was born near Pocomoke City in Somerset County, Maryland, on August 29, 1815. She was the first child of Thomas King Carroll, a descendant of two prominent Maryland families, the Protestant Kings and the Catholic Carrolls. Charles Carroll, the patriarch of that family, had been attorney general under the third Lord Baltimore. One of his grandsons, Charles Carroll of Carrollton, was the only Roman Catholic signer of the Declaration of Independence, as well as the longest surviving signer. He lived long enough to become one the founders of the Baltimore and Ohio Railroad in 1827.

The Eastern Shore Carrolls were Protestants and members of the Episcopal Church, a fact that would figure in Anna Carroll's career. Her father owned Kingston Hall, a thirteen-hundred-acre tobacco plantation in Somerset County. He was politically active, had served as a judge, was a member of the House of Delegates and was governor of Maryland in 1830–31. Anna was the eldest of nine children and was her father's favorite. He had her tutored at home and trained her to be his aid, a rather progressive step for the time. She read all the books in her father's library, including his extensive collection of works on American and foreign law.

At age fifteen, during her father's term as governor, Anna was sent to Miss Margaret Mercer's boarding school for girls in West River, Maryland, to finish her education. Mercer was a governor's daughter too, and also had been taught by her father. Her curriculum concentrated not only on training her students for the "woman's sphere" of home and family, but also offered courses in the sciences, philosophy and religion.[1] Mercer was also an abolitionist. But Mercer did not agree with many Northern abolitionists who believed in eliminating slavery by force. Although Anna left the school after only one year, she had absorbed Mercer's abolitionist views, including the idea that slavery should not be forcibly ended.

Thomas Carroll, like many planters, was land-rich but cash-poor. Moreover, he was a poor financial manager and his resources quickly dwindled. As judgments and creditors' lawsuits mounted, Carroll sold many of his slaves and finally lost Kingston Hall in 1837.

Anna had tried to help with the family finances by opening her own school, but it closed it in 1843, when the family moved to Church Creek in Dorchester County. Anna Carroll never married. Probably because of her family's distressed financial condition, she decided to make her living in the world of public affairs with her pen.

By 1845, she was in Baltimore, where she used her father's political and business connections to get work as a writer for commercial enterprises. Even through the profession of public relations consultant hadn't yet been invented, that was, in effect, what she had become. She maintained a fact-finding service for shipping and railroad companies and lobbied for them in Washington. She wrote promotional pamphlets and legislative reports and gathered investment information. She also wrote articles on political subjects for local newspapers.[2]

Carroll entered the national political arena in the 1850s, after she had successfully lobbied Whig President Zachary Taylor to appoint her father as naval officer for the district of Baltimore. In 1854, she joined the nativist American Party (more commonly known as the Know-Nothings), following the demise of the Whigs. The Know-Nothings, who were anti-immigrant and anti-Catholic, had been formed as a reaction to the flood of immigrants (many of them Catholic) from Ireland and Germany in the 1840s. But the party was also antislavery and pro-labor, making it appear to be the most progressive political influence in Maryland at the time.

During the 1856 presidential election, Carroll actively campaigned for Millard Fillmore, the American Party candidate. Maryland was the only state Fillmore carried. During the campaign, Carroll wrote a book elaborating on the Know-Nothing platform, the anti-Catholic *The Great American Battle, or, The Contest Between Christianity and Political Romanism*. The book warned against the danger of papal power in the United States and the influence

Anna Ella Carroll

Anna Ella Carroll. *Courtesy of the Maryland Historical Society.*

of Catholic schools, and pronounced in favor of restricting immigration.[3] Carroll became the chief publicist for Thomas Holliday Hicks, who credited his 1857 election victory as Maryland's governor to her efforts.

When Lincoln was elected in 1860, Carroll freed her slaves and devoted her writing to opposing Southern secession and preventing Maryland from seceding. She advised Governor Hicks on compromise efforts to ensure Maryland would remain within the Union. Carroll acted as liaison between Governor Hicks and Lincoln and wrote several unsigned newspaper articles to rally public support in Maryland for the Union.[4] She has also been credited with sending intelligence on pro-secession plans within the state to Washington.

In the spring of 1861, Senator John C. Breckinridge of Kentucky had charged in a speech on the Senate floor that Lincoln had violated the Constitution by mustering state militias into service after the assault on Fort Sumter, suspending habeas corpus and imposing martial law and a naval blockade of the South. Breckinridge had been James Buchanan's vice-president, and in 1860 he had run against Lincoln as a Southern Democrat. He later became a Confederate general and the Confederacy's last secretary of war.

Breckinridge repeated his speech to an audience in Baltimore, and Carroll was incensed that he was attempting to stir up secessionist sentiment in the state. She wrote a detailed response to Breckinridge's speech, "Reply to the Speech of the Honorable J.C. Breckenridge," which she had printed at her own expense and circulated. The Lincoln administration and the War Department were pleased with her reply, and they circulated it at government expense. At the urging of the administration, she wrote two more "propaganda" pieces in support of the administration's war measures, "The Relationship of the National Government to the Revolted Citizens Defined" and "The War Powers of the Federal Government."

In "War Powers," Carroll's closely reasoned arguments display the education in the law and politics she had received from her father. In it, she marshaled an impressive list of legal authorities to argue that the president's war powers as commander in chief had ample precedent in American and international law. Those powers included the authority to suspend habeas corpus. However, she cautioned the administration to avoid the temptation to approve the confiscation acts being proposed in Congress. Confiscating Southern property (including slaves) as a war measure might be sound legally, but it was bad politics. If the administration's theory was that the conflict was a "rebellion" and not a war against a foreign enemy, then the Constitution was still in force in the

South and Southerners were entitled to its protections. Moreover, she argued, confiscation would be a bad political signal to those Southerners working for reconciliation with the Union and would harm the administration in the Northern and border states.[5]

Carroll never received the payment for her writing she had been promised. She claimed in a letter to Lincoln that an assistant secretary in the War Department had made an oral promise to pay her $50,000 for her documents, but the secretary left the administration and her claims for compensation fell on deaf ears after his departure.[6]

The most controversial part of Carroll's wartime career has to do with her alleged role as a military strategist. She always claimed, and many people have agreed, that she initiated and convinced the War Department to approve the "Tennessee Campaign" for invading the Confederacy in the western theatre. Prior to Carroll's plan, the War Department's strategic thinking had concentrated on splitting the Confederacy by invading the South with a gunboat expedition via the Mississippi River. However, the plan had many logistical and tactical problems, since major sections of the Mississippi running through the Confederacy were heavily defended and fortified.

The story goes that in September 1861, Lincoln sent Carroll on a fact-finding mission to the West. In St. Louis, she met with General John C. Fremont, then commander of the Western Department. She also met with several pro-Southern citizens, whom she charmed into telling her what they knew about the defenses and navigability of the rivers running through the South. She also met with a riverboat pilot, who gave her information about what rivers could handle gunboats.

Armed with this information, Carroll presented the War Department with a plan that concentrated on an invasion using the relatively undefended Cumberland and Tennessee Rivers. Convinced of the logic and practicality of Carroll's plan, the War Department shifted its strategy. Fort Henry on the Tennessee was taken on February 6, 1862, and Fort Donelson on the Cumberland fell on February 16. Ulysses S. Grant became an overnight hero.

Carroll also supposedly argued that the army and navy should concentrate next on Vicksburg and Mobile. She presented detailed plans and maps that demonstrated the utter futility of trying to take Vicksburg from the river and that only a land assault from the rear of the city would succeed. Grant ignored her advice, and his march through the swamps and sloughs north of Vicksburg failed. It was only when Grant allegedly saw the wisdom of her plan and marched his army south and east, investing Vicksburg from the rear, that he was victorious.

Carroll continued to advise the government and wrote Union propaganda during the rest of the war. After Lincoln's assassination and the first years of Reconstruction, she was largely ignored. In 1870, she filed a claim with Congress for compensation and recognition for her war efforts, but she was rebuffed. A bill to grant her recognition and a government pension was introduced in the House in 1881. Unfortunately, before the bill could be heard, President Garfield was assassinated, and Carroll's bill disappeared from the congressional agenda. In 1885, Carroll filed a lawsuit against the government for compensation, but the United States Court of Claims held that there was simply no legal evidence to support her claim for military services.[7]

By this time, Carroll's health had deteriorated, as had her financial condition. She turned to her relations, the Catholic Carrolls, for help. But her earlier anti-Catholic writings for the Know-Nothings guaranteed that she would receive a cool reception, and she was turned down.

Many people believed her claims and lent assistance to gain her the recognition they felt she deserved. She became a cause for the suffragists—the feminists of the time—who claimed that Carroll would have been successful in Congress if women had been allowed to vote. Sarah Blackwell's *A Military Genius: Anna Ella Carroll of Maryland* (1891) set the framework for a feminist campaign that continues to this day.

Much of the writing about Carroll over the years accepts without question the proposition that she would have been recognized for her efforts but for her gender. The mindset of the time would not permit the Lincoln administration and the War Department to let it be known that much of the Union strategy in the West had originated with a woman. Field commanders would not have followed orders they knew had been based on plans developed by a civilian, let alone a "lady."

An interesting example of Carroll's legendary status as a "shadow" member of Lincoln's inner circle comes from a painting on display in the U.S. Capitol in Washington. The 1864 painting, *The First Reading of the Emancipation Proclamation* by Francis Bicknell Carpenter, depicts Lincoln reading the Proclamation to his cabinet. At the extreme right of the table around which Lincoln and the cabinet members are gathered is an empty chair, containing only the kind of maps and reports Carroll supposedly carried with her when she met with administration officials. Legend has it that the maps and reports in the empty chair symbolize Carroll and her unacknowledged influence within the government.

But the "empty chair" legend has no documentary support, and Carroll's proponents neglect to mention how ironic the claim really is. Carroll had opposed the Emancipation Proclamation, believing it would injure Union support in the Northern and border states. Instead, she favored colonization for African Americans and advocated a scheme to transport freed slaves to Central America.

Recent studies have looked at the evidence for her military claims and have reached mixed conclusions. One professional scholar believes the evidence does not support Carroll's claim of being the originator of the Tennessee Campaign. She concludes that Carroll's reputation as a military strategist is vastly overblown at best; at worst, it is a myth.[8] A more recent study by a nonprofessional historian[9] is more charitable to Carroll, but promises more than it delivers in terms of new evidence or a convincing reinterpretation of existing sources.

Without question, Carroll was an extraordinary person and a role model for later generations of women. Her decision to pursue a career in the "man's world" of Victorian America was courageous. Her political work and writings played a significant role in underpinning the Lincoln administration's case to the American people. Whether her contributions in the military sphere—the basis for much of her present fame—are valid remains an open question.

Carroll died in 1894 and is interred in the Carroll family plot at Old Trinity Church near Church Creek in Dorchester County. Her epitaph reads, "A woman rarely gifted; an able and accomplished writer." Later were added the words,

> *Maryland's Most Distinguished Lady. A great humanitarian and close friend of Abraham Lincoln. She conceived the successful Tennessee Campaign and guided President Lincoln on his constitutional powers.*

Carroll's gravesite is listed in the *Maryland Women's Heritage Trail*.[10]

CAMP PAROLE

Outside Annapolis, across Solomons Island Road from the old Parole Plaza Shopping Center and the rising towers of the Annapolis Towne Centre, stands a lonely historic marker. The marker states (somewhat ungrammatically) that

> located in this vicinity, [is] one of three camps established during the Civil War to accept paroled Union prisoners of war until they were exchanged for Confederate prisoners similarly confined in the South, over the course of the war. Thousands of soldiers were held here until they were returned to their regiments or sent home. Many who did not survive are buried in Annapolis National Cemetery.

The marker speaks of one of the more obscure chapters of the war. When the war began, neither the North nor the South implemented a formal system for exchanging prisoners. President Lincoln refused to ask Congress for a declaration of war because he believed that would be tantamount to recognizing the Confederacy as a separate nation. Nor did Lincoln want to grant the seceding states any of the traditional rights under the international and military laws of warfare.

That was to change in July 1861, when the Confederates captured a large number of Federal soldiers at the First Battle of Bull Run (Manassas). Congress requested that Lincoln take measures to ensure the prisoners would be exchanged. Up to that time, opposing commanders occasionally arranged informal exchanges of prisoners under a flag of truce, but all such arrangements were ad hoc and discretionary.

The first government-sanctioned prisoner exchange took place in February 1862, but it was not until July 1862 that a formal "cartel" detailing

Camp Parole, Annapolis, historical marker.

the exchange system between the Union and the Confederacy was agreed upon. Each side appointed commissioners who would administer the system. Under this agreement, all prisoners were to be released—either exchanged or paroled—within ten days of capture.

An equivalency table was devised according to which a fixed number of enlisted men would be exchanged for an officer:

1 general=46 privates
1 major general=40 privates
1 brigadier general=20 privates
1 colonel=15 privates
1 lieutenant colonel=10 privates
1 major=8 privates
1 captain=6 privates
1 lieutenant=4 privates
1 noncommissioned officer=2 privates.[1]

Prisoners who could not be exchanged immediately were to be released "on parole," meaning they could not perform any military duties until they were officially notified that they had been exchanged. "Parole" is French for "word." Being "paroled" meant that a soldier gave his written "word of honor" that he would abide by the terms of his release from captivity.

However, it soon became apparent that many paroled men, once released, would go home and simply disappear into the civilian population. It became difficult, if not impossible, to force them to rejoin their units after they had been officially exchanged. Word of the parole arrangement soon spread through both armies, and there were reports of soldiers voluntarily surrendering so that they would be paroled and sent home.

The Federal government sought to deal with this problem by creating "parole camps." Camp Parole was established in Annapolis by War Department General Order No. 59 on June 5, 1862. The idea was to keep paroled soldiers under military discipline and in a known place, where they could be quickly sent back to their units when they had been officially exchanged.

The camp was designated a "camp of instruction" for fifty thousand men. The "camp of instruction " designation meant that the camp also served as an induction and boot camp, but in fact its principal purpose was to serve as a holding place for paroled soldiers pending their exchange. The Annapolis camp was established to hold parolees from New England and the middle states. Other parole camps were established at Jefferson Barracks (Camp Benton) south of St. Louis and Camp Chase near Columbus, Ohio. These other parole camps were also instruction camps and later served as prison camps for captured Confederates. Camp Parole in Annapolis probably escaped becoming a prison camp because of its proximity to Camp Hoffman at Point Lookout, which opened in 1863.[2] Local legend in Annapolis has it that there were Confederate prisoners of war in the parole camps, but there is no evidence that that was the case.

The first Camp Parole in Annapolis was located near College Creek at the rear of the campus of St. John's College. It was called College Green Barracks. Paroled prisoners, sometimes in groups as large as six thousand, were brought up the Chesapeake to Annapolis by steamer. The prisoners were required to bathe before entering the camp. Their clothes and shoes were thrown into College Creek, where decades after the war their leather boots were still being pulled from the mud.[3]

Eight wooden barracks had been erected on the campus, each meant to house 150 men.[4] But the influx of so many paroled men soon made facilities woefully inadequate. The land by the creek was low and drainage was poor, making parts of the camp miserable in wet weather. Hospital facilities and the camp guard were inadequate, despite the commandant's frequent pleas to Washington. When there was no more room in the barracks, men lived in tents or in huts they built themselves from lumber stolen from public

St. John's College, Annapolis, the site of the first parole camp for Union soldiers.

buildings. It is estimated that 70,000 men passed through the Annapolis parole camps, although the camp population was probably never more than 7,000 at any one time.[5]

To deal with the overcrowding, the War Department abandoned the St. John's College site and a second parole camp was established close to where Solomons Island Road crosses the South River. This site allowed steamers to unload parolees directly into the camp. Soon, however, there were complaints from local farmers, whose fences were disappearing because parolees wanted to make wooden floors for their tents. As garbage and debris piled up, the War Department decided this site was inadequate also.

On May 1, 1863, the Federal government signed a lease with Charles S. Welch and his wife for the use of their 250-acre farm west of Annapolis that became the final Camp Parole. The new site was about two miles from the Annapolis and Elkridge Railroad station. Later, a station was built at the camp itself. The new site was a good one, because the Annapolis and Elkridge connected with the B&O Railroad's Washington Line at Annapolis Junction, meaning parolees could be sent by rail from any location the Federals controlled.

By mid-December, forty-nine of the eighty-three authorized buildings were occupied. But conditions remained grim for the "inmates," particularly the wounded. The staff surgeon complained that the 168-bed hospital was totally inadequate for the 6,570 men then in the barracks. He recommended adding two more wards and a washhouse to improve sanitation.

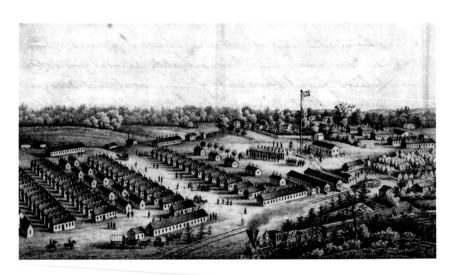

Camp Parole in Annapolis, circa 1864. *Courtesy of the Maryland State Archives.*

Wounded or sick parolees remained as hospital patients until they were able to travel or died. Many of the dead remained in Annapolis and are interred in the local national cemetery, established in 1862. The Annapolis National Cemetery is the final resting place not only for the Camp Parole dead, but also for those who died in Annapolis's two other military hospitals at St. John's College and the grounds of the U.S. Naval Academy.

Identifying the dead was a major problem during and after the war. At that time, soldiers did not have government-issued "dog tags" or seldom wore or carried any other means of identification. If a wounded soldier was left behind or separated from his unit, couldn't speak or was unconscious and had no means of identifying himself (such as letters from home), he might easily die a stranger to those who attended to him. Clara Barton came to Annapolis after the war and assisted with identifying many of the unknowns lying in the National Cemetery.

Life must have been hard and full of boredom for the parolees waiting to be exchanged. Their days were filled with endless drill. Diversions were few, although it has been said that the parolees started a camp newspaper (the *Skirmisher*) and many played baseball, a relatively novel game in Annapolis at the time. Some of the parolees may have been hired out as laborers to local farmers.[6]

As the conflict continued and was transformed from a war of limited objectives into "total war," the parole system broke down and was eventually discontinued. The Confederacy reacted violently to Lincoln's Emancipation Proclamation and the enlistment of black troops. Reacting to news that the Union intended to enlist colored troops, Jefferson Davis issued a general order in 1862 that captured colored troops and their white officers would not be exchanged or paroled, but instead, they would be put on trial for "inciting servile insurrection." There were reports of captured white officers being executed and black troops being sold into bondage.[7] In July 1863, Lincoln issued an order, stating that for every Union soldier killed in violation of the laws of war, a Rebel soldier would also be killed; for every soldier enslaved or sold into slavery, a Rebel soldier would be placed in hard labor.[8] Lincoln later relented, and his retaliatory order never went into effect. But prisoner exchanges and paroles slowed dramatically after the Confederacy's directive and became one reason the Federal government initially hesitated at using black troops in combat.

Moreover, the Union eventually realized that the Confederacy could not replace soldiers who had been killed, severely wounded or captured. The Confederacy's ill-fated gamble on liberating the prisoners of war at the Point Lookout prison camp in St. Mary's County in July 1864 is further evidence of the South's increasingly desperate manpower situation.

Exchanged prisoners were the South's last hope of adding soldiers to its armies. Finally, in August 1864, General Grant formally ended all prisoner exchanges. The action made sense from a strategic military standpoint, but it was a cruel blow to those prisoners who now could not look forward to being exchanged or going home.

Thus began one of the grimmest chapters of the war—the rapid increase and expansion of the prisoner of war camp system. The horrors of Andersonville and the Andersonville equivalents in both the North and South soon followed.

Camp Parole was closed on July 18, 1865. Today, nothing remains of any of the camps except the lonely historical marker. A Mrs. Tucker, who was postmistress of the village of Parole in the 1920s and '30s, said that from her girlhood until about 1915, it was a common sight to see an old man get off the train at Parole Station. He would wander about the village and fields as though in some time past he had been there before. Some local would remark, "Another old soldier come back." And so it was—an old veteran back to visit once again before he died one of the less spectacular scenes of the most thrilling four years of his life.[9]

POINT LOOKOUT

Point Lookout, located on a peninsula at the confluence of the Potomac River and Chesapeake Bay, is the southernmost point of land on Maryland's Western Shore. The site's recorded history extends as far back as Captain John Smith's journals. The land was once part of St. Michael's Manor, one of three properties owned by Leonard Calvert, the first governor of the Maryland colony.

In the years leading up to the Civil War, the site had become a fashionable summer resort, replete with around one hundred beach cottages, a hotel, a large wharf and a lighthouse. The war, which was to change much in Maryland, transformed this pleasant spot into what would become the Union's largest prisoner of war camp and, arguably, the worst in the North.

The Point Lookout resort fell on hard times as the war curtailed visitors. The owner defaulted on his mortgage, and the Baltimore mortgage holder offered the site to the U.S. government. The War Department leased the resort to build a hospital to care for the growing number of Federal casualties. Named Hammond General Hospital, it received its first Union army patients on August 17, 1862. The army built the hospital—twenty buildings in total—in a circular shape, like spokes on a wheel.

Early in 1863, Federal authorities ordered a small number of civilian Confederate sympathizers from Southern Maryland to be confined on the hospital grounds. Southern Maryland was heavily pro-Confederate, and a number of Federal troops had been dispatched to St. Mary's and Charles Counties to keep watch on the population and interdict people and supplies from crossing the Potomac to assist the Confederacy.

The Battle of Gettysburg changed the fate of Point Lookout dramatically. After the battle, the Union army found itself with more prisoners than it

Map of Point Lookout and Camp Hoffman prisoner of war camp. *Courtesy of the Maryland Historical Society.*

had planned for. Point Lookout was deemed close enough to transport prisoners from the Gettysburg and Virginia battlefields, yet was isolated enough to make escape difficult. The Federals expanded Hammond Hospital's grounds and established Camp Hoffman—probably named after Colonel William Hoffman, the Federal commissary general of prisoners—to house ten thousand prisoners of war. Three forts were erected to protect the prison. A rail line was laid linking Washington with Point Lookout, which later became the Southern Maryland Railroad.

Camp Hoffman was designed to house enlisted prisoners only. Most Confederate officers who were sent there were later transferred to Fort Delaware, located on an island south of Wilmington. As the war progressed, the camp population dramatically increased. In September 1863, four thousand Confederates were being held in the camp; by December, the number had increased to nine thousand. By the following June, less than one year after the camp was built, there were more than twenty thousand prisoners.[1]

A board fence enclosed the twenty-three-acre camp, which consisted of six wooden buildings that served as dining halls and kitchens. The prisoners lived in tents year-round. Living conditions were grim, since the exposed geography of the point meant that winters were extremely cold and the summer heat was oppressive. Camp Hoffman housed several

Point Lookout prisoner of war camp, St. Mary's County, historical marker.

Confederate soldiers who had come from St. Mary's County, but their families were forbidden from aiding the prisoners with the food, clothing and medicine so badly needed on the sometimes freezing, sometimes burning, fever-ridden split of sand that was Point Lookout.[2]

An inspector from the U.S. Sanitary Commission noted in November 1863 that Camp Hoffman's grounds and quarters were filthy. The prisoners were ragged, dirty and poorly clothed. There was only one blanket for three men. Prisoners were periodically forced to vacate their tents while authorities checked for "surplus" blankets. After these searches, many prisoners found that their personal possessions had been taken. The prisoners had to forage for their firewood, and there was never enough. Prisoners complained they didn't get enough food.[3] Conditions didn't measurably improve as the war went on.

Diseases were rampant. The most common were scurvy and chronic diarrhea. The camp's hospital facilities were limited to eighteen tents, and the conditions were abominable. The serious cases were moved to Hammond Hospital.[4] A smallpox hospital stood across Lookout Creek north of the camp.

About 52,000 Confederate prisoners passed through the camp during its two years of operation; 3,384 documented prisoners died and are buried there. Due to haphazard record keeping, the number of documented dead is probably low. One author has put the total at over 4,000.[5] These figures do not include about 300 civilians, mainly captured blockade runners and Southern sympathizers. All the bodies were buried in shallow graves, which had to be moved about twenty years later due to soil erosion along the Chesapeake. The graves were moved a third time to the present site of the Confederate monument.

Camp Hoffman has the dubious distinction of having the highest mortality rate of any Union prison camp. The death rate at Point Lookout was probably between 25 and 28 percent, exceeding the death rates at camps at Elmira, New York (24 percent), and Rock Island, Illinois (17 percent). In contrast, the death rate at Andersonville was 29 percent and at Salisbury, North Carolina, it was 34 percent.[6]

The Point Lookout hospital and camp also served as a gathering point for runaway slaves. Several doctors and nurses at Hammond Hospital gave refuge to Southern Maryland slaves fleeing bondage before Maryland formally abolished slavery in late 1864. Thousands of "contrabands" (escaped and captured slaves) were transported to Point Lookout from Virginia, where they were given food and shelter at a camp established outside the prisoner of war compound. Many contrabands enlisted in United States Colored Troops regiments. Several USCT soldiers were assigned to guard the Confederate prisoners.

Today, two monuments honor the memory of the prisoners who died at Point Lookout. The State of Maryland dedicated the first in 1876. The U.S. government dedicated a second monument in 1911, which lists the names of the then-documented Confederate dead. In 1965, a hundred years after the conclusion of the war, the Maryland State Forest and Park Service began to develop the site that is today Point Lookout State Park, which now comprises 1,064 acres.

BARBARA FRITCHIE OF FREDERICK AND NANCY CROUSE OF MIDDLETOWN

"Shoot, if you must, this old gray head
But spare your country's flag," she said.
—John Greenleaf Whittier, "Barbara Frietchie," 1863

There was a time in the not-too-distant past when schoolchildren used to memorize and recite John Greenleaf Whittier's stirring ballad "Barbara Frietchie," the patriotic poem commemorating the feisty ninety-five-year-old widow from Frederick, Maryland, who allegedly confronted Stonewall Jackson and defiantly refused to take down her U.S. flag.

The poem certainly had far-reaching impact. For example, on May 17, 1943, Franklin Delano Roosevelt and Winston Churchill were driving through Frederick en route to Shangri-La (which President Eisenhower renamed Camp David) for the weekend. Churchill noticed a sign advertising the Barbara Fritchie "Candy Stick" Restaurant (which still exists). The Fritchie (the common spelling, also sometimes Frietchie or Freitschie) reference triggered schoolboy memories for both world leaders. Roosevelt could remember only a few lines of Whittier's poem, but Churchill jumped in and recited the entire ballad from memory.[1]

This episode speaks to the enduring power of the written word, but begs the question—is the Barbara Fritchie story true?

Barbara (née Hauer) Fritchie was born in Lancaster, Pennsylvania, in 1766, the daughter of immigrants who had come to Pennsylvania from the Palatine in Germany in 1754. She married John Casper Fritchie, a glover, in 1806. She is said to have been a friend of Frances Scott Key when he practiced law in Frederick. Fritchie's husband, many years her junior, operated his glove-making business out of their small brick house on West Patrick Street. He died in 1849.

Fritchie's alleged heroics occurred during Robert E. Lee's 1862 Maryland Campaign, which culminated with the Battle of Antietam (Sharpsburg). The Army of Northern Virginia had occupied Frederick on September 6, and on the morning of September 10, Jackson's Second Corps was marching out of the town to assault the Federal garrison at Harper's Ferry. One of Jackson's soldiers reportedly spotted a Union flag hanging from the upstairs window of Barbara Fritchie's house. According to the ballad, Jackson ordered his men to fire on the flag. Just as the flag was about to fall from its staff, Fritchie snatched it up, stood at the windowsill and spoke her immortal words of defiance to Jackson. Shamed and moved by her courage, Jackson ordered his men to leave the old woman and her flag alone and march on.

People began questioning the Fritchie-Jackson story almost immediately after the poem appeared. According to an alternate version, Fritchie was sick in bed that day and couldn't have come to the window. She told her housekeeper to hide the valuables to prevent the soldiers from looting them and to take in the Union flag hanging outside. But the housekeeper forgot about the flag, and Confederate troops shot it up.

Jacob Engelbrecht, the son of a Hessian soldier imprisoned in Frederick during the Revolution who chose to remain there after the war, lived across the street from Fritchie. From 1818 until 1882, Engelbrecht kept a detailed diary of events large and small in Frederick City. Engelbrecht's diary recorded Fritchie's ninety-fifth birthday and other events, but said nothing about the flag incident. In fact, an entry in his diary from 1869 states,

> I would here remark that the "Barbara Fritchie" exploit, as put in poetry by…Whittier…is not true. I do not believe a word of it. I live directly opposite, and for three days I was nearly continually looking at the Rebel army passing the door and nearly the whole army passed our door and should anything like that have occurred I am certain someone in our family would have noticed it.[2]

Despite Engelbrecht's claim that the entire Rebel army passed his door, another supposed fact that belies the Fritchie story is Jackson's line of march on the day the flag incident supposedly took place. His corps was proceeding north up South Benz Street that day and then was to turn left at West Patrick Street to march out of town. To pass Fritchie's house, Jackson's corps would have had to turn right and march east, back into town. Fritchie's house was over one hundred feet east of Benz Street and across a bridge over Carroll Creek. So, if the "line of march" claim is true, it is doubtful that any of Jackson's men ever passed her door.

The Barbara Fritchie House in Frederick.

And Jackson himself reportedly was visiting a Presbyterian minister at the time and not traveling with his troops. Henry Kyd Douglas, a Marylander whom a historian has recently "outed" as the most likely person to have lost the famous copy of Lee's Special Orders No. 191 before the 1862 Maryland battles,[3] claimed he was with Jackson every minute the general was in Frederick. Douglas swore that Jackson neither saw nor spoke to Fritchie—nor she to him.[4]

What does seem true is that Fritchie waived her flag when General Ambrose E. Burnside's Federal corps marched through Frederick on the twelfth. And according to a *New York Times* article, a Mrs. Mary Quantrell later wrote to Whittier in 1863 and 1876, claiming that she was the "real" Barbara Fritchie and asked him "to do her justice." She had energetically waived her flag, but Jackson and his troops had ignored her. An entry in Jacob Engelbrecht's diary for August 1, 1879, notes the death of "Mrs. Mary Quantrill [*sic*], the original B. Fritchie."[5]

Perhaps the final word on the incident should come from the poet himself. John Greenleaf Whittier (1807–92) was a Massachusetts-born writer of Quaker lineage who also edited abolitionist newspapers. One of Whittier's biographers states that the poet first heard of the Fritchie incident from a Mrs. Emma D.E.N. Southworth, the "well-known novelist" of Georgetown, D.C., in July 1863. She wrote him a description of the incident "which went around the Washington papers last September," including some additional details she later heard from friends who had been in Frederick at the time.[6] So, in fact, Whittier based his understanding of the events on thirdhand summaries from newspaper accounts and reports from friends of a friend.

Answering his critics as to the accuracy of the reports, Whittier later wrote an explanatory note stating that the poem

> *was written in strict conformity to the account of the incident as I had it from respectable and trustworthy sources. It has since been the subject of a good deal of conflicting testimony, and the story was probably incorrect in some of its details. It is admitted by all that Barbara Frietchie was no myth, but a worthy and highly esteemed gentlewoman, intensely loyal and a hater of the Slavery Rebellion, holding her Union flag sacred and keeping it with her Bible; that when the Confederates halted before her house, and entered her dooryard, she denounced them in vigorous language, shook her cane in their faces, and drove them out; and when General Burnside's troops followed close upon Jackson's, she waved her flag and cheered them. It is stated that May [sic] Quantrell, a brave and loyal lady in another part of the city, did wave her flag in the sight of the Confederates. It is possible that there has been a blending of the two incidents.[7]*

Barbara Fritchie died on December 18, 1862, at age ninety-six, three months after the incident that would make her name famous in the North. She is interred in Mount Olivet Cemetery in Frederick, where her grave, near that of her friend Francis Scott Key, remains a tourist attraction. Whittier's entire sixty-line ballad is written on her monument. Fritchie's flag can still be seen at the Barbara Fritchie House and Museum at 154 West Patrick Street in Frederick. The house was damaged by the flooding of Carroll Creek in 1868 and was moved several feet east and rebuilt from the remaining materials.

War, it seems, produces legends and myths of tenuous truth, some of which catch on and are perpetuated because they boost morale and strike a patriotic chord. It is highly probable the Barbara Fritchie story is one of them.

Not every Maryland flag story was mainly the stuff of legend. Another incident, this one true as well as deadly, occurred during Jubal Early's 1864 raid in Maryland. Confederate General Bradley Tyler Johnson ordered Colonel Harry Gilmor, a Baltimore County native, to take 135 men and ride

U.S. flags at the present Nancy Crouse house in Middletown.

into Harford County to destroy the Philadelphia, Wilmington and Baltimore Railroad's bridge at Magnolia Station. The troopers reached Magnolia Station on July 11, partially destroyed the bridge and wrecked two trains.

Earlier that day, Gilmor's advance guard had passed the home of Ishmael Day in Fork, Maryland. Day, a Union sympathizer, had hung a large Union flag across a road on a rope, knowing that Gilmor's troops would be passing by. A sergeant in the advance guard, Eugene Fields, demanded that Day take the flag down. Day refused, an argument ensued and Day shot Field at close range with a shotgun. Fields died soon after, and Gilmor's men burned Day's house to the ground. Day survived by hiding in some woods until Gilmor's troops had passed by.[8]

Although fated to be perpetually eclipsed by the Barbara Fritchie/Frederick legend, the Nancy Crouse flag incident in nearby Middletown during Lee's 1862 Maryland campaign is well documented and apparently actually happened. The Confederate army entered Middletown on September 10 and 11, and quickly discovered that the town was strongly pro-Union. As Stonewall Jackson rode through the town, two girls with ribbons of red, white and blue floating from their hair and small Union flags in their hands, rushed out of their house and ran to the curb, laughingly waving their flags

The Nancy Crouse house in Middletown (not the original).

in Jackson's face. Their horrified mother quickly bustled the girls back into the house. "We evidently have no friends in this town," Jackson said quietly to his staff after bowing and doffing his cap to the girls.[9]

A seventeen-year-old saddler's daughter named Nancy Crouse had a large American flag hanging from her second-story bedroom at her home on Main Street. A dozen Confederate cavalrymen stopped to pull it down and were met by Nancy and a friend, Effie Titlow. The girls asked what the men wanted. "That damned Yankee rag," replied one of the soldiers.

Nancy raced up the stairs and returned to her front porch with the flag draped around her body. She reportedly said, "You may shoot me, but never will I willingly give up my country's flag to traitors." One of the cavalrymen pointed a pistol at her, and at that point Nancy understandably changed her mind and gave up her flag. The trooper rode away with the flag tied around his horse's head.

When pursuing Federal cavalry entered Middletown and heard Nancy's story, they galloped after the Confederates in a rage, captured most of them and gave Nancy's flag back to her.[10]

Both the Nancy Crouse House at 204 West Main Street and Barbara Fritchie's house are part of the Maryland Women's Heritage Trail.

However, Nancy Crouse's original house was moved to the back of the lot around 1900, pulled down and replaced with the present structure.[11] The owners still prominently display U.S. flags.

And perhaps it is only "poetic" justice that a young woman who was one of the "real" Barbara Fritchies should also have had a ballad composed in her honor:

Honor to the Maryland maid,
Who the banner saved that day
When thro' Autumn sun and shade
Marched the legions of Gray;
Middletown remembers yet
How the tide of war was stay'd
And the years will not forget
Nancy Crouse, the Valley Maid.[12]

THE UNIVERSITY OF MARYLAND AND THE CIVIL WAR

The University of Maryland, College Park, is considered the state's flagship public institution of higher education. It has been called a "public Ivy," a university that provides an Ivy League collegiate experience at a public school price.[1] But despite its world-class reputation today, the college from which the university grew barely survived the Civil War, due in part to events during and after the war that tainted the school as a "nest of treason."

The origins of the University of Maryland lie with the aristocratic Baltimore Farmer's Club, later renamed the Maryland State Agricultural Society. The members talked about creating a college where their sons could learn gentlemanly values and engage in scientific research, and where their poorer neighbors could learn to "work harder" and acquire a trade or profession.[2]

The society's leader was Charles Benedict Calvert, a descendant of the Barons Baltimore, a relative of six Maryland governors and a future U.S. congressman. Calvert had attended the University of Virginia (where his classmate was Edgar Allan Poe), and dreamed of creating a similar school of higher learning in Maryland. On March 6, 1856, the forerunner of today's University of Maryland was chartered as the Maryland Agricultural College. Two years later, Calvert purchased 420 acres of the Riverdale Plantation and founded the school with money earned from the sale of stock. On October 6, 1859, the first thirty-four students entered the college, including four of Calvert's sons.

In July 1862, the same month the college awarded its first degrees, President Lincoln signed the Morrill Land Grant Act. The legislation provided Federal funds to schools that taught agriculture, engineering or provided military training. Taking advantage of the opportunity, the college became a land grant institution in February 1864, after the General Assembly gave its approval.

Ironically, the Morrill Act and the contemporaneous Homestead Act, which offered cheap Western land to homesteaders, only became law after the departure of Southern legislators from the U.S. Congress in 1861. The acts had been proposed before the war, but Southern congressmen had blocked them because they considered the legislation a threat to the expansion of slavery in the territories.

A few months after becoming a land grant institution, the college found itself in the middle of the war. In April 1864, General Ambrose E. Burnside and six thousand soldiers of the Federal Ninth Corps camped on the college campus en route to reinforcing the Army of the Potomac in Virginia. While encamped, Burnside's troops tore down several hundred feet of fence for firewood and tried to set fire to a stone barn. The college sued the Federal government for damages, but the lawsuit was unsuccessful.

Later that summer, an event occurred that lives on in local legend, though its veracity is doubtful. The legend goes that on the night of July 12, 1864, a large force of Confederate cavalry and infantry, mostly Marylanders, stopped at the college, and the pro-Southern faculty and gentry of Prince Georges County threw a party for the officers, a fête that was dubbed the "Old South Ball."

The backdrop for the so-called Old South Ball was Jubal Early's 1864 raid on Washington. In July, General Robert E. Lee sent fifteen thousand men under General Jubal Early to attack Washington. The principal objective was to take pressure off the Army of Northern Virginia, then under siege around Petersburg, by forcing the Federal army to send troops north to defend the capital.

Early crossed from Virginia into Washington County, Maryland, and quickly marched to Frederick. He "ransomed" the city for $200,000 in cash.[3] At the Monocacy River on July 9, he engaged a smaller force under the command of General Lew Wallace, who had rushed from Baltimore to delay Early until Federal reinforcements arrived from Virginia. Outnumbered three to one at the Monocacy, Wallace was defeated and withdrew, but his timely action allowed elements of the Federal Sixth and Nineteenth Corps to rush to Washington by steamer. The troops arrived just in time to secure the capital's defenses.

Believing the road was clear to Washington after Wallace's retreat, Early gave an extraordinary order to his cavalry commander, General Bradley Tyler Johnson. General Lee had a secondary objective for the Maryland raid. Johnson was to proceed north of Baltimore to destroy railroad and telegraph links with the North. He then was to pass east and south of Washington and attempt to reach Point Lookout in St. Mary's County, where a Union prisoner of war camp held thousands of Confederate prisoners.

As is mentioned elsewhere in these essays, by 1864 the Confederacy was critically short of military men. An attempt to liberate thousands of Confederate prisoners might seem a desperate but—under the circumstances—reasonable gamble. Lee had hoped that Johnson's operations in Central Maryland would force the Federals into moving the Potomac Flotilla closer to Washington to defend the capital. He had arranged for Jefferson Davis to send Confederate vessels from Wilmington, North Carolina, into the open Potomac. The vessels would assault Point Lookout with a battalion of Confederate marines and arm the prisoners of war. Johnson was to take command of the enlarged force and link up with Early to assault Washington.

Johnson was an excellent choice for the mission. A native of Frederick, Maryland, he had practiced law there, been a state's attorney and was a former chairman of the Maryland Democratic Party. His great uncle, Thomas Johnson, had been the first governor of the state after independence. The men under his command included the Second Maryland Cavalry and the Baltimore Light Artillery. Johnson's men were certain they would be warmly received in heavily pro-Confederate Southern Maryland.

Johnson's troops entered Prince Georges County on the morning of July 12. Their first objective was to disrupt rail traffic around Laurel and then head to Upper Marlboro and Southern Maryland. However, scouts reported Federal cavalry around Laurel, so Johnson led his men south toward Beltsville. At Beltsville, the Confederates tore up railroad tracks and captured five hundred mules, which they hoped to use to transport prisoners from Point Lookout back to Washington.

Johnson had just re-formed his column to continue the march, when he received a message from Early. Johnson was ordered to abandon the Point Lookout expedition and join Early in Silver Spring. Early had assaulted Forts Stevens and DeRussy in the District of Columbia earlier that day, and had been repulsed by the veteran Federal troops who had just arrived from Virginia. He had decided to abandon the Maryland incursion. Early would wait for Johnson in Silver Spring until 9:00 p.m.

As it happened, Early's order was fortuitous for another reason. Richmond newspapers had published reports about the Point Lookout expedition and Confederates feared Federal intelligence agents had learned about it. Consequently, the element of surprise had vanished and Jefferson Davis had recalled the ships and marines. Thus, the effort to rescue the Confederate prisoners was doomed from the start.

Brigadier General Bradley Tyler Johnson, CSA. *Courtesy of the Maryland Historical Society.*

Johnson's column marched down the Washington Turnpike (now U.S. Route 1) to the Maryland Agricultural College. College president Henry Onderdonk came out to meet the Confederates, possibly to find out their intentions or to make sure that the troops would not inflict the same kind of damage Burnside's soldiers had caused not long before.

Around 5:00 p.m. Johnson set up headquarters at the residence of a faculty member, now the Rossborough Inn. Johnson apparently intended the stop at the college to be a resting and gathering point for his troops before undertaking the ten-mile march to link up with Early in Silver Spring.

The lead elements of Johnson's column set out around 7:30 p.m. and barely made it to Silver Spring by 9:00 p.m., Early's deadline. Johnson himself did not reach Silver Spring until after midnight.

Despite this somewhat hectic timetable, the legend persists that Johnson's officers were entertained at the college well into the night at the Old South Ball. For many years after the war, small squares of land were preserved at places around the campus where guards were said to have been posted around the site of the ball. Although some reports placed the site at the Rossborough Inn, that isn't likely—the building was a private home at that time. A more likely place was the Old Main Building, where some of Johnson's soldiers may have been served—or may have taken—some food.

As one student of the episode has remarked, balls usually involve preplanning, and it wasn't known until after 2:00 p.m. that Johnson's men would be stopping at the college.[4] And once Johnson received his new orders from Early, his officers surely would have been preoccupied with assembling their men and making ready to march onward.

Moreover, there are no contemporary written records of a ball. Diarist Florida Clemson, who lived in nearby Riverdale and was a granddaughter of John C. Calhoun, attended many functions at the college during that period, but her diary is silent about a ball. After the war, Johnson and two of his officers wrote about the Washington raid, but none of them made any reference to a ball and barely mentioned stopping at the college.[5]

In July, an agent of the Federal Judge Advocate General's Corps investigated the incident to determine if anyone at the college had been openly disloyal to the Union. He interviewed several witnesses. Some passersby reported that they thought they had heard music and had seen carriages carrying ladies heading for the college. It was determined that some people from the community had visited with Johnson during the afternoon and that several young daughters of faculty members and staff had been present. Someone from the college or the cavalrymen themselves could have provided music. However, there was no conclusive documentary evidence that a ball ever took place.[6]

Rossborough Inn on the campus of the University of Maryland, one of the possible sites of the "Old South Ball."

The report went on to state that although the college was indeed a "nest of rebels," it could not be established that Johnson's arrival had been planned for or that the college had prepared food for the Confederates. The investigator concluded that it was more likely that Johnson's men had simply taken over the college and helped themselves to whatever food they could find.[7]

Did the Old South Ball ever take place? Were the locals trying to emulate the so-called "Sabres and Roses Ball" that J.E.B. Stuart hosted at the Landon House in Urbana before the Battle of Antietam in September 1862? We will probably never know. But as one writer put it, after all the inconclusive facts have been evaluated,

> *the final ingredient is the chemistry between flashy Maryland cavaliers in their grey uniforms with red capes and the daughters of staff and faculty. Cavalrymen were the rock stars of their day. Thus, from a combination of young girls and dashing cavaliers whose average age was 19 was born the story of the Old South Ball.*[8]

Whatever the truth of the matter, stories about the Old South Ball and the taint of treason haunted the school for several years. The public furor forced President Onderdonk to resign.

Then, college officials compounded the problem with a series of gaffes. When the war ended, the college was struggling to survive. To meet expenses, the trustees sold off two hundred acres of land— now the College Park shopping area and College Heights Estates.[9] In an effort to curry favor with the pro-Southern gentry and attract their sons as students, the trustees offered the presidency to George Washington Custis Lee, a son of Robert E. Lee and himself a former Confederate general. The General Assembly, then controlled by pro-Unionists, was not favorably impressed, and it admonished the trustees with a resolution stating that the college, by making the Lee appointment, had proved itself "a[n] unsafe place for the education of our young men" and not worthy of state or Federal support.[10] More politically astute than the trustees, General Lee declined the post and later succeeded his father as president of Washington College in Lexington, Virginia, later to become Washington and Lee University.

The conservative trustees continued hoping to attract conservative planters' sons, but their families were too cash-poor to pay tuition. They appointed another president, who failed to attract students. The college was on the brink of disappearing.

The presidency was then offered to an ex-Confederate Marylander, Admiral Franklin Buchanan. Buchanan accepted the post, cut tuition and dramatically increased enrollment. But slashing tuition put the college in debt, and his imperious conduct soon led to his resignation.[11]

In 1864, Libertus Van Bokkelen, a Baltimore Episcopal priest, former president of St. John's College and an ardent crusader for public education, envisioned a comprehensive plan for a state school system capped by a state university. His scheme to combine the Baltimore medical and law schools, Washington College in Chestertown, St. John's College in Annapolis and the Maryland Agricultural College into a unified state university failed when all but the Maryland Agricultural College backed out of the plan.[12]

The Maryland Agricultural College grudgingly agreed to state affiliation, no doubt propelled by its precarious financial condition and the taint of the Old South Ball. It would take nearly a century before the Maryland Agricultural College would become the keystone of the statewide public university system that is today's University of Maryland.

RICHARD SEARS MCCULLOCH

THE CIVIL WAR'S "CHEMICAL ALI"?

We tend to think of terrorism as a modern phenomenon, but in fact its origins, theory and practice are centuries old. Scholars inform us that the very word "terrorism" stems from the French Revolution.[1] Since 9/11, increased attention has been paid to the history of terrorism. Surprisingly, the Civil War provides some startling examples. There is evidence that weapons of mass destruction (WMDs), notably biological and chemical agents, were not only proposed during the war, but may have actually been tried.[2]

An obscure Maryland academic proposed some of the most potentially devastating WMDs during the Civil War. Richard Sears McCulloch is one of the war's more elusive figures, but recent research has shed light on his wartime activities and what might have been his deadly contribution to the Confederacy in its waning months.

McCulloch was born in Baltimore in 1818 and was raised on the family farm, "Oldfields," near Glencoe in Baltimore County. His father, James William McCulloch, occupies his own small place in history as the chief teller of the Baltimore branch of the Second Bank of the United States. When the Maryland General Assembly imposed a tax on banks not chartered by the state (an obvious attempt to cripple the unpopular federally chartered institution), McCulloch sued the state on the bank's behalf. The case was appealed to the Supreme Court of the United States and resulted in one of Chief Justice John Marshall's most famous decisions, *McCulloch v. Maryland*.[3]

Richard attended a private school in Philadelphia and graduated from the College of New Jersey (now Princeton University) in 1836 at the age of eighteen. His mentor at Princeton was the chemist Joseph Henry, who is credited with inventing a forerunner of the electric motor and was the first secretary of the Smithsonian Institution.

After graduation, McCulloch taught natural philosophy (the physical sciences of physics and chemistry) at colleges in Pennsylvania. In 1846, he married Mary Stewart Vowell of Alexandria, Virginia, a cousin of Robert E. Lee. McCulloch then accepted a position with the United States Mint in Philadelphia, where in 1849 he invented an inexpensive method of refining the gold ore pouring into the East from California. He was dismissed from the Mint, possibly for attempting to patent his gold-refining discovery, and became a professor of natural philosophy at Princeton.

In 1854, McCulloch was appointed professor of natural and experimental philosophy and chemistry at Columbia College in New York. In September 1863, two months after Gettysburg and the New York City draft riot, he abruptly resigned from the Columbia faculty, writing to the college president from Richmond that "it should encite [sic] no surprise [sic] that one, born and reared a southerner, prefers to cast his lot with that of the South."[4]

McCulloch's resignation was widely publicized in the North and did little to enhance Columbia's reputation. The New York Copperheads (peace Democrats), including apparently some influential members of the Columbia community, may have played a role in the July draft riot.[5] Whether McCulloch was in league with the local Copperheads or had a hand in the draft riot isn't known, but he had refused to sign an unofficial loyalty oath that the college had circulated after the riot.

The trustees were furious with McCulloch and refused to accept his resignation. Instead, they expunged his name from the faculty records, an action reminiscent of the treatment resigning U.S. naval officers received before going south.[6] George Templeton Strong, the noted Civil War diarist, was a Columbia alumnus and a college trustee. He wrote that McCulloch

> has "gone over to the dragons" and we are well rid of him. He has probably been offered a high price to come south and take charge of some military laboratory.[7]

Strong wasn't too far off the mark. Armed with a fistful of recommendations from academics loyal to the South, McCulloch was recommended for a post at the Confederacy's Nitre and Mining Bureau as a consulting chemist. The bureau's principal task was to oversee the mining of compounds for explosives and to ensure a steady supply of nitre (saltpeter), an essential component of the black powder used in muskets, handguns, cannon charges and "torpedoes" (naval mines).

McCulloch was happy to be of use, but lobbied hard for a military commission. He reasonably concluded that a military rank would give him more protection under the laws of warfare, especially if he were captured. Family tradition has it that he received the rank of colonel or general, but Confederate records that survive cannot confirm this.

McCulloch had an important reason for trying to protect himself under the cover of a military commission. What records do survive indicate that McCulloch became a member of the Confederate clandestine services, one of several agents reporting directly to Jefferson Davis and Judah Benjamin, then Confederate secretary of state. Benjamin's operatives included the Montreal group that planned the raid on St. Albans, Vermont, attempted to set fire to hotels in New York City and one of whose number met with John Wilkes Booth on at least one occasion.[8]

It appears from the evidence that McCulloch perfected two chemical weapons. The first was an improved form of "Greek fire," an inflammable compound that would self-ignite. Confederate agents had used an earlier version in the attempt to set fire to the New York hotels but had failed—by placing the material in small hotel rooms with the windows shut, all the available oxygen was rapidly consumed and the fires quickly went out.

In February 1865, McCulloch developed a form of lethal gas that could be used as an antipersonnel weapon. McCulloch's formula and laboratory notes have been lost, but it is speculated that he had developed a form of the oxygen-consuming gas halon, or possibly a form of chlorine or cyanide gas.[9]

McCulloch demonstrated the new weapons to a small delegation of Confederate legislators. He shut up a number of cats in a room in his Richmond laboratory and poured a vial of a colorless liquid on the floor. Within a few minutes, all the cats were dead. McCulloch said that if the liquid "were thrown from the gallery of the House of Representatives in Washington, it would kill every member of the House in five minutes."[10] He then demonstrated his improved "Greek fire" by dipping a handkerchief in his formula and placing it on a mantelpiece. After a few seconds, it burst into flame.[11]

It is unknown whether the Confederacy ever seriously considered using McCulloch's gas as an antipersonnel weapon. However, one of the Confederate legislators who had witnessed the demonstration, W.S. Oldham, enthusiastically recommended use of the improved "Greek fire" to Jefferson Davis. He wrote to Davis that

> [t]here is no necessity of sending persons in the military service into the enemy's country…the work might be done by agents, and in most cases by persons ignorant of the facts, and therefore innocent agents…We can 1. Burn every vessel that leaves a foreign port for the United States 2. We can burn every transport that leaves the harbor of New York or other

Northern port with supplies for the armies of the enemy in the South. 3. Burn every transport and gun boat on the Mississippi River, as well as devastate the country of the enemy, and fill his people with terror and consternation.[12]

The war ended before the Confederacy could put McCulloch's weapons into practice against Northern military or civilian targets. After Richmond fell, McCulloch fled with several other members of Davis's administration.

He was captured in Florida before he could make his way to Cuba. McCulloch initially appeared to be of little importance, but one of the witnesses at the trial of the Lincoln conspirators reported finding records in the Confederate archives alluding to McCulloch's chemical weapons. He was placed in solitary confinement in Libby Prison in Richmond while Federal authorities looked for evidence that his weapons had been used. It has been mentioned that one of the reasons for searching for actual uses of McCulloch's WMDs was to provide evidence sufficient to justify hanging Jefferson Davis. Curiously, one of McCulloch's prison diversions was sketching cats, his former "laboratory subjects."

In March 1866, McCulloch was released and paroled to New York. He soon received an offer to teach, which he accepted. His cousin-in-law, Robert E. Lee, had in the meantime become president of Washington College (later Washington and Lee University) in Lexington, Virginia. Lee convinced the college trustees to offer McCulloch a professorship of natural philosophy, and he stayed on the faculty until 1877. In 1876, a collection of his lecture notes was published in book form, *The Mechanical Theory of Heat and the Steam Engine*, which became a pioneering work in the field of thermodynamics. McCulloch later held a professorship at the Louisiana State University, but he left in 1884. He died in 1894 at his family's home near Glencoe, Baltimore County.

Desperate situations sometimes lead to desperate measures. It is fortunate that the war ended before the Confederacy was faced with the decision whether to initiate "state-sponsored terrorism" on a massive scale.

THE 1864 CONSTITUTION

MARYLAND ABOLISHES SLAVERY

Belair [Md.] *Aug 25ᵗʰ, 1864*

Mr president [Lincoln,] *It is my Desire to be free, to go to see my people on the eastern shore. My mistress wont let me*[. Y]*ou will please let me know if we are free, and what I can do.*
                                   —*Annie Davis (Harford County slave)*[1]

The Civil War produced many changes in Maryland, but it is hard to think of a more profound transformation than how a state that might have joined the Confederacy in 1861 if left to its own devices would become the first border state to abolish slavery three years later.

Annie Davis's letter was forwarded to the War Department, but she never received an answer. Her confusion is understandable, since when she wrote her letter some slaves in the South were free but many others, including those in the border states, were not.

In November 1862, Marylanders went to the polls to elect a governor and delegates to the General Assembly. The federal government had dispatched troops to the state to protect Union sympathizers and ordered all secessionists returning from Virginia and appearing at the polls held prisoner until after the election.[2] Harford County native Augustus W. Bradford was elected governor. The new House of Delegates was overwhelmingly pro-Union. Bradford and the new legislature campaigned on and stood for a platform with only two positions—Union and slavery. But ominous winds were blowing from Washington.

On September 22, 1862, President Lincoln issued an executive order declaring that slaves in those states "in rebellion" and not returning to the United States by January 1, 1863, would be free. A second executive order issued on January 1, 1863, specified the states and areas in which his earlier order would apply. The two executive orders combined are what we call the Emancipation Proclamation.

The Emancipation Proclamation had little initial impact. It purported to free only those slaves outside of the reach of the Federal government within the seceding states. And it specifically did not apply in the border states of Missouri, Kentucky, West Virginia, Maryland and Delaware or those parts of the Confederacy (sections of Virginia, Louisiana and Tennessee) then under Federal military control. So the answer to Annie Davis's question was no—she was not free. She lived in Maryland, a state specifically exempted from the Emancipation Proclamation. Commenting on this ironic situation, Secretary of State William H. Seward supposedly acidly remarked that

> *We show our sympathy with slavery by emancipating slaves where we cannot reach them and holding them in bondage where we can set them free.*[3]

Many people still think the Emancipation Proclamation was merely political propaganda or a diplomatic gambit to prevent Britain, France and other countries from formally recognizing the Confederacy. But it was more than that. It set the Federal government on a path that would lead to the total eradication of slavery, and Maryland would play an important role in that effort.

In July 1862, Congress had passed and Lincoln signed a confiscation act, declaring that all property seized from persons assisting or engaging in rebellion against the United States would be forfeited. The act specifically applied to slaves. The first slaves to benefit from the Emancipation Proclamation and the confiscation act were the so-called "contrabands," Southern slaves who had escaped from bondage and made their way to Union-held territory or those whom the military had taken from their owners.

In April 1862, the Lincoln administration floated a proposal to compensate slave owners for the value of their slaves if they freed them. The border states rejected the offer. Many Marylanders, in particular, were reluctant to add the 87,189 slaves to the large and supposedly dangerous free African American population of 83,942.[4] On June 19, 1862, Congress mandated compensated abolition in the District of Columbia, which ended slavery there.

The cumulative effect of the compensation offer, the Emancipation Proclamation and the abolition of slavery in the District of Columbia put enormous pressure on Maryland slaveholders. Many slaves in counties bordering the district ran away to find sanctuary in Washington. Other

William Augustus Bradford, governor of Maryland (1862–66). *Courtesy of the Maryland Historical Society.*

slaves sought refuge in Federal enclaves such as Hammond Hospital and Camp Hoffman at Point Lookout.

Governor Bradford attempted, with some success, to force the Federal government to return fugitive slaves, but the increasing contradictions between supporting the Union and maintaining slavery were becoming apparent. He fought an increasingly desperate effort to hold together his coalition, which was splitting into abolitionist and conservative factions. The slaveholders themselves were in a quandary. They could no longer sell their excess slaves to the Deep South, a very profitable source of revenue before the war. The growing antislavery sentiment in Maryland was quickly making their "capital" in slaves—estimated to be worth $30 million at the start of the war—worthless.

Ultimately, the abolitionist faction won out and determined that the only viable course was emancipation. They prevailed on Bradford to call for a convention to draft a new state constitution that would mandate emancipation. The convention met in Annapolis between April 27 and September 6, 1864. The constitution was submitted to the voters on October 12 and 13. Soldiers were sent to polling places to ensure that the voting was fair and voters would not be intimidated. Election judges were instructed to administer an oath of allegiance to the United States before permitting voters to cast ballots. Maryland Union soldiers in the field were permitted to vote where they were stationed. Despite many claims to the contrary, it has never been conclusively proven that the Federal military interfered with the vote.

The voters approved the new constitution by the narrowest of margins. Out of a total of 59, 973 votes cast, the constitution was approved 30,174 in favor to 29,799 against, or 50.31 percent.[5] Citizens voting in their usual polling places opposed the constitution by 29,536 to 27,541. Maryland's Union soldiers had provided the crucial votes for passage, approving the constitution by 2,633 to 263. The new constitution went into effect on November 1.

In addition to abolishing slavery, the 1864 constitution contained a number of interesting features. It abolished religious tests for voting, created the office of lieutenant governor and reapportioned voting districts for the General Assembly based on the white population only. The latter provision was an effort to diminish the political power of the small counties where the majority of the state's former slave population lived and reduce the power of Southern sympathizers. By design, the constitution disenfranchised Marylanders who had left the state to fight for or live in the Confederacy. It made it difficult for them to regain full rights of citizenship and required office holders to take a new oath of allegiance to support the state and the Union.

On October 12, as Marylanders were going to the polls to vote on the new constitution, Roger Brooke Taney died. His death was perhaps the crowning symbol of the passing of the old order. What would the author of the *Dred Scott* decision have thought? In fairness to him, he had always maintained that slavery was a state, not a Federal issue, and that each sovereign state could legislate its own solution if it chose. So perhaps the old jurist would have been satisfied.

Maryland's path to emancipation differed greatly from the other border states. Missouri abolished slavery in January 1865 after a constitutional convention ratified an 1864 emancipation proclamation by its governor. The counties that broke away from Virginia in 1862 were admitted into the Union as the new state of West Virginia on condition that the state's constitution provide at least for the gradual elimination of slavery. Kentucky and Delaware never abolished slavery, but passage of the Thirteenth Amendment made their inaction moot. Concerned that the Emancipation Proclamation was merely a war measure that had no permanent legal effect, Congress proposed the Thirteenth Amendment to the Constitution in January 1865 to end slavery once and for all. The amendment went into effect on December 18, 1865, when the requisite number of states had ratified it. Maryland ratified the Thirteenth Amendment on February 3, 1865. Delaware finally ratified the amendment in 1901, having rejected it in February 1865. Kentucky did not ratify until 1976, having also rejected it in February 1865. Mississippi finally ratified on March 16, 1995.

Maryland's efforts at "self-reconstruction" were generally successful—they prevented the more heavy-handed approach the Federal government used in the seceding states. But the results were far from satisfactory for the freedmen. In 1867, Conservative Democrats regained control of the General Assembly. A new state constitution was proposed and approved in September. The 1867 constitution (Maryland's present one) abolished the office of lieutenant governor[6] and revised the apportionment formula to include blacks, thus reinstating power to the smaller and rural counties. The General Assembly failed to approve the Fourteenth Amendment to the Constitution (granting citizenship to free blacks) and the Fifteenth Amendment (granting voting rights). In 1910, the so-called Digges amendment to the state constitution attempted to impose property requirements for voting. This was a bald attempt to disenfranchise black voters, and it was rejected at the polls.

In an effort to regulate the large numbers of newly emancipated "free labor," Maryland Democrats soon passed a series of "black codes" that defined the role of free blacks. To ensure white control, these laws required that all adult black males had to be employed by a white person.

Any blacks who were unemployed were declared vagrant and subject to arrest. These measures, as well as others adopted in Maryland and many Southern states over the years, soon led to the Jim Crow era and segregation. Not until the civil rights statutes and U.S. Supreme Court cases of the 1950s and '60s would the reality of emancipation for the freed African Americans be fully realized.

H.L. MENCKEN AND
THE CIVIL WAR

H.L. Mencken had an opinion on practically everything. So it is not too surprising that the "Sage of Baltimore" had a few things to say about the Civil War and its impact on Maryland and the South.

Editor, columnist, essayist and critic, Henry Louis Mencken (1880–1956) was a writer of enormous national influence who played a leading role in American intellectual life in the first half of the twentieth century.[1] A native of Baltimore, where he spent virtually all of his life, he was an editor and columnist for the *Baltimore Evening Sun*, a contributor to *The Smart Set* and a founder of the *American Mercury*. His book, *The American Language*, is a classic study of what made American English so distinctive and more dynamic than its British parent.

Heavily influenced by satirists such as Jonathan Swift and Mark Twain, Mencken's principal trait was skepticism—about religion, democracy and adherents to middle-class values (people he called the "booboisie").

Mencken conducted a crusade against American provincialism, Puritanism and prudery—traits, as his biographer Fred Hobson notes, he found, to a larger degree, to exist in the states below the Potomac and Ohio Rivers.[2] Mencken considered the South he knew, roughly the four generations after the Civil War, to be a wasteland. "It is as sterile, artistically, intellectually, culturally, as the Sahara Desert."[3] As he believed he had demonstrated in his famous coverage of the 1925 Scopes Monkey Trial in Tennessee and numerous essays, nothing but "anthropoids" populated the lower South and the Appalachian region.

Mencken's style was notable for its hyperbole and bombast, but his writing usually reflected his real feelings. His feelings about the South were actually rather complex, particularly since, as a Marylander, he considered himself a Southerner of sorts. How he came to his opinions is interesting, because he believed that the Southern "intellectual vacuum" he observed was a direct result of the Civil War.

He wrote that life in America would have been much pleasanter if the Union had been dissolved and the South had won the Civil War.[4] What at first blush seems like a startling opinion from an alleged hater of Southern ways makes sense in context. What had happened, in his opinion, was that "the vast blood-letting of the Civil War half exterminated and wholly paralyzed the old aristocracy, and so left the land to the harsh mercies of the poor white trash."[5] In 1917, he had written that in Virginia,

> *the best of the South today, all was crassness. A Washington or a Jefferson dumped there today would be denounced as a scoundrel and jailed overnight…*
>
> *It would be impossible in all history to match so amazing a drying-up of civilization. I say a civilization because that is what, in the old days, the South had, and it was a civilization of manifold excellences, and lavish fruits. Down to the middle of the last century and even beyond, the main hatchery of ideas in America, despite the pretensions of the Yankees, was below the Potomac. It was there that all the political theories we still cherish were born; it was there the gentler adornments of life were cultivated. A certain noble spaciousness was in the Southern scheme of things. It made for reflection, for tolerance, for the vague thing we ineptly call culture.*[6]

His article, "The Calamity of Appomattox," which appeared in the *American Mercury* in 1930, is illustrative. In it, Mencken speculates (as many others have done) on what would have happened had the South won the war. The chief evil of the Union victory, he wrote, was a victory of "the Babbits" over what used to be called "gentlemen." The chief theory behind the Confederacy was an essentially aristocratic view of the world. If the South had won, their government would have been founded on a concept of human inequality, with a superior minority at the helm.[7] Mencken strongly supported such an arrangement.

> *Even in politics, the old specialty of the South, there is an astounding collapse. In the early days Virginia led the nation; today Virginia is content to tag along after the brummagem uplifters of the middle West, bawling for prohibition, populism, all the claptrap of Bryanism. On the theoretical side the politics of the State is imitative, childish, almost idiotic. On the practical side it is cheap, ignorant, dishonest—a mere matter of rival gangs of jobseekers struggling for the salary teat. Both sides make indecent bargains with the Anti-Saloon League rabble rousers. Neither side can show a man capable of leadership.*[8]

H.L. Mencken (1880–1956). *Courtesy of the Maryland Historical Society.*

Abraham Lincoln, he believed, was a parvenu and a humbug. Lincoln had become

> *the American solar myth, the chief butt of American credulity and sentimentality. Like William Jennings Bryan, he was a dark horse made suddenly formidable by fortunate rhetoric.*[9]

As a connoisseur of American English, Mencken gave Lincoln mixed praise for the Gettysburg Address, judging it "eloquence brought to a pellucid and almost gem-like perfection. But let us not forget that is poetry, not logic; beauty, not sense."[10]

Mencken considered Lincoln's speech highly ironic and, from a Southern standpoint, ridiculous. The theory of the Gettysburg Address, he maintained, is simply that the Union soldiers who died at Gettysburg sacrificed their lives for the cause of self-determination.

> *It is difficult to imagine anything more untrue. The Union soldiers… actually fought against self-determination; it was the Confederates who fought for the right of their people to govern themselves. What was the practical effect of the battle of Gettysburg? What else than the destruction of the old sovereignty of the States…The Confederates went into the battle free; they came out with their freedom subject to the supervision and veto of the rest of the country—and for nearly twenty years that veto was so effective that they enjoyed scarcely more liberty, in the political sense, than so many convicts in the penitentiary.*[11]

Mencken's gloss on the Gettysburg Address shows his strong affinity with the "Lost Cause" theory. He apparently found "government of the people, by the people and for the people" repugnant. Contempt for democracy was a constant theme in his writing.

The immigrants to Maryland whom Mencken admired most hadn't come from Europe, but rather they had come from across the Potomac in the years following the Civil War. He believed that Southerners, particularly Virginians, embodied the best of nineteenth-century America. They had come to Baltimore in large numbers to restart their lives. The exhausted and "occupied" South during Reconstruction gave them little opportunity to resume their previous lifestyle. Before the war, the planter class's wealth had been overwhelmingly concentrated in land and slaves. That wealth, which permitted a leisure class to cultivate the very kind of lifestyle Mencken so highly praised, was gone. The land had been devastated and African Americans were no longer anyone's "capital."

Maryland was "Southern" enough for these immigrants to feel at home and among people who shared their values. Many of them believed Maryland had shown, and retained, strong pro-Southern sympathies.

Whether it was from an expression of pure pro-Southern sentiment or, more likely, from a discernment of a rare business opportunity, it is undoubtedly true that Maryland prospered in the postwar years by becoming the South's preferred financial partner. Maryland capital virtually rebuilt the devastated South in the roughly four decades following the war. Investment banks such as Alexander Brown and Sons; Wilson, Colston and Co.; and Middendorf, Oliver and Company had underwritten investments in Southern railroads, steamship lines, utilities, cotton mills, coal, iron and phosphate mines and lumbering enterprises.[12] Southern states and municipalities turned to "Southern" Baltimore instead of "Yankee" New York, Philadelphia and Boston to underwrite their bonds. Baltimore commercial banks, such as the Safe Deposit and Trust Company and the Mercantile Trust, made significant loans to Southern businesses.[13] By 1900, Maryland investment in the South stood at about $100 million.[14] Baltimore was to the South what Chicago was to Midwest prosperity and what San Francisco was to growth on the Pacific coast.[15]

Mencken felt that the Virginians, and to a lesser extent the "best people" from the other Southern states, did more for Baltimore than any other group.

> *My own native town of Baltimore was greatly enriched by their immigration, both culturally and materially; if it is less corrupt today than most other large American cities, then the credit belongs largely to the Virginians, many of whom arrived with no baggage except good manners and empty bellies.*[16]

The white Southern migration to Maryland is a documented fact, and these "internal immigrants" quickly began to play a leading role in Maryland's economic, social and cultural life in the postwar period. Others have echoed Mencken's belief that Baltimore became "the poor house of Virginia" (and other parts of the South) after the war.[17]

To cite but a few examples, William Meade Dame of Danville, Virginia, had enlisted in the Confederate army at age sixteen and served as an artilleryman with the Richmond Howitzers. His forty years as rector of Memorial Church in Baltimore and his chaplaincy of the Fifth Regiment, Maryland National Guard, earned him the title "Bishop of Bolton Street."[18]

Sidney Lanier, the poet and ex-Confederate from Macon, Georgia (and a prisoner of war at Point Lookout), joined the Peabody Symphony Orchestra and lectured on poetry at Johns Hopkins. He wrote some of his best lyric poems while living in Baltimore.

Basil Lanneau Gildersleeve, the subject of another chapter in this volume, came to Baltimore via Charleston and the University of Virginia and became one of the country's most distinguished scholars and man of letters during his forty years at John Hopkins.

Colonel David Gregg McIntosh, a native of South Carolina and one of the best artillery commanders in the Army of Northern Virginia, settled in Towson after the war. He practiced law, became head of the state bar association and founded Towson's oldest bank.

Richard M. Venable, from Charlotte County, Virginia, came to Baltimore after the war with little more than a letter of recommendation from Robert E. Lee and started a law practice. The firm that bears his name is one of largest in the state. Venable served as a Baltimore city councilman and was president of the Board of Park Commissioners.

Charles Marshall, a native of Fauquier County, Virginia, was a great nephew of Chief Justice John Marshall. He had come to Baltimore before the war to open a law practice. He went back to Virginia when the war started and was on Robert E. Lee's staff as his military secretary. Marshall returned to Baltimore after the war and practiced with the law firm that would later become Piper and Marbury, now DLA Piper.

What is curious is the question of why Mencken would idealize and identify with the planter class. Clearly, Mencken was an elitist who purportedly believed in a "natural aristocracy." But the Virginians and older Marylanders of the planter class were precisely the group with which the descendants of German immigrants like Mencken had the least in common. Marylanders and Virginians who came to dominate Baltimore's political and social institutions in the late nineteenth and early twentieth centuries were primarily of English descent. Mencken hated the British, and openly supported Germany before America's entry into World War I. He had many positive things to say about Nazi Germany before Hitler's expansionist agenda became too blatant to excuse. As a proud German, Mencken constantly vilified the "Anglo-Saxon" ruling class in America. The world of Baltimore's elite—the horse farms, foxhunts and balls—was completely foreign to him.

Part of the answer to this paradox lies with Mencken's perception of his own German roots. The branch of the family with whom he most closely identified (though he wasn't a direct descendant) had been lawyers, judges and professors at the Universities of Leipzig, Wittenberg and Halle in the seventeenth and eighteenth centuries. When he came across a book one of his ancestors had written in 1715 satirizing his fellow professors, Mencken wrote, "It gave me a great shock. All my stock in trade was there—loud assertions, heavy buffooneries, slashing attacks…It really was uncanny."[19]

The Virginians and older Marylanders were gentlemen and modeled their lives after the English country gentry. They were schooled in the art of living, good food and drink and a civilized leisure. The old Tidewater planters had inquiring minds, lived ordered lives and embraced a religious skepticism—precisely the qualities Mencken believed his ancestors possessed. Indeed, Mencken wrote that he "belonged" to the eighteenth century, with its sense of order, predisposition toward reason, religious skepticism and an emphasis on conduct, manners and being a gentleman. It was an Enlightenment world of order and civility, and it was no coincidence that the eighteenth century was also the period in which Mencken's forebears had flourished. The antebellum Tidewater planters were the last aristocrats in a land overrun with democracy. When Mencken praised their world, he felt he was praising the world of his own fathers.[20]

Today, Mencken's contempt for democracy, belief in a natural aristocracy and a government and culture dominated by a leisure class elite seem quaint, almost like exhibits in a museum. Many people considered him a fossil even before his death. American politics, society and culture had taken a decidedly more inclusive turn even before the Civil War highlighted the increasing isolation of a Southern culture almost feudal in nature. Events in Europe and the United States had ensured the ultimate triumph of democracy even before Mencken was born. Landed aristocrats would have to adapt to the new realities or perish.[21] Nor did Mencken's naïve idealization of a pastoral, serene antebellum South agree with the reality that other writers, including Southerners, have documented. Like many of the Southerners he praised, Mencken's real "civil war" was a war against modernity.

Nevertheless, Mencken's views have recently undergone a sort of revival. One occasionally finds favorable comments about him from ultraconservatives and advocates of the "Southern heritage" movement in the blogosphere. But few of his contemporary disciples seem to comprehend his sense of satire or that he exaggerated his case to make his points.

Most surprising, especially to Mencken, was the reaction his writing received in the South. After the initial shock and vituperation subsided, many Southerners admitted that they agreed with him, and young writers in particular were quick to respond to the substance of his attack. Accordingly, he has been credited with providing the impetus to the Southern literary revival that began during his lifetime. Mencken later conceded that Southerners were beginning to produce high-quality literature and thought, and he encouraged and assisted those efforts.[22]

It is intriguing to think about what a politically incorrect, verbal bomb-thrower like Mencken would have become had he lived in our time. Would a twenty-first-century Mencken have forsaken traditional journalism and literature and become a TV "talking head" or a radio "shock jock"? Would he have become a spokesperson for a mass audience? It is doubtful. More likely, he would have considered the modern media culture just as contemptible as the postbellum Southern culture he had vilified. After all, today's political, media and entertainment elites are not "gentlemen" by his standards and more closely resemble the "booboisie."

In the final analysis, Mencken is unique and defies categorization. One suspects that his idea of a "natural aristocracy" was based more on nostalgia than conviction. The entire body of his writings demonstrates that Mencken's notion of an aristocracy was not really centered on social class, but rather, on a kind of a meritocratic elitism. For Mencken, the only true aristocracy was the aristocracy of the mind.

MARYLAND'S STATE FLAG AND RECONCILIATION

Maryland's is one of the most distinctive and recognizable state flags in the United States. But it is not generally known that the Civil War is largely responsible for its design and that the design symbolizes the reconciliation of Marylanders who fought for the North and the South.

Unique among the fifty states, Maryland's state flag derives from medieval English heraldry and depicts the coat of arms of Maryland's founding family. The design is from the shield of George Calvert, the first Lord Baltimore, who applied for a charter and land grant to what is now Maryland from King Charles I.

George Calvert and his wife reputedly both came from the English gentry, and each family had its own arms. Calvert's shield, according to the Maryland secretary of state, combined the black and yellow colors from his father's family with the red and white (more authentically "sable" or silver) colors from his mother's family, the Crosslands.

The first and third quadrants feature alternating black and yellow colors, while the second and fourth quadrants feature alternating red and white colors forming a "cross buttony," a cross with a "trefoil" (three buds) on each end. According to one theory, since Calvert's mother, Alicia Crossland Calvert, had no brother, she was heiress to her family's estate. Under heraldic law, she was permitted to quarter her arms with her husband's.

The Crossland family connection has, however, been disputed. Dr. Edward C. Papenfuse, the Maryland state archivist, claimed in a 1995 lecture[1] that the red and white cross buttony pattern actually derives from the arms of the Mynnes, George Calvert's wife's family. When Calvert was elevated to the Irish peerage in 1625, he incorporated the cross buttony and the color red from Ann Mynne's family's coat of arms. The Mynne arms appear on Anne Mynne's tomb in England and prominently feature a cross buttony. The Mynne arms are also well documented in the local country history where the Mynnes lived.

Papenfuse also claims that there is no conclusive evidence that Alicia Crossland Calvert actually came from the same family that had been awarded the Crossland arms. In 2000, a Maryland state senator introduced a bill to correct the historical record along the lines Papenfuse suggested. However, since the College of Arms in London does not adequately document the granting of Irish peerages and the related heraldry, there was no way to prove conclusively the origin of the red and white cross buttony pattern.[2] The bill was withdrawn, and Maryland still officially recognizes the second and fourth quadrants of the state flag as deriving from the Crossland family arms.

Throughout the colonial period, only the black and yellow Calvert family colors are mentioned in descriptions of the Maryland flag. The black and yellow colors also became closely associated with the city of Baltimore, and still appear prominently on the city's flag.

Probably due to a superabundance of republican spirit after independence, the "aristocratic" Calvert colors and arms disappeared from the state's great seal and flags. However, in 1854 a new great seal was introduced that revived the use of the Calvert arms, although they were relatively inconspicuous in the overall design. Various flags were used to represent the state, although the General Assembly never officially adopted a design. The most common state flag in the nineteenth century probably consisted of the great seal of the state on a blue background, as is common with many other state flags today. These blue banners appear to have been used at least until the late 1890s.

The Civil War, ultimately, was to change the state flag dramatically. Probably because the black and yellow "Maryland colors" or "Baltimore colors" were popularly identified with a state that had remained in the Union, Marylanders who sympathized with the South adopted the red and white cross buttony from the Crossland arms as their colors. Following Lincoln's election, red and white "secession colors" began to appear on everything from stockings and cravats to children's clothing. Federal authorities vigorously prosecuted people who displayed these red and white symbols of resistance to the Union.

During the war, Maryland-born Confederate soldiers used the red and white cross buttony design as a unique way of identifying their place of origin. Pins in the cross buttony shape were worn on uniforms, and the headquarters flag of General Bradley T. Johnson was a red cross buttony on a white field.

The red and white Crossland colors continued to be associated with Confederate Marylanders after the war. The monument on Culp's Hill at the Gettysburg battlefield honoring the Confederate Second Maryland Regiment bears a cross buttony on each side. The Maryland Line Confederate Soldier's Home, established in Pikesville in 1888, featured a large cross buttony on its service badges, invitations to events and other regalia.

By the end of the war, both the black and yellow and the red and white cross buttony colors were clearly identified with Maryland, although they represented opposing sides. As soldiers returned home after the war, the greatest challenge facing a deeply divided state was reconciliation, where Confederates who had fought under the red and white "secession colors" had to be reintegrated into a state that had stayed within the Union.

As the process of healing took place in the post–Civil War era, a new symbol began to appear. A flag of alternating quadrants of the Calvert and Crossland colors began to be displayed at pubic events. Neither the designer nor the date of origin of this new Maryland flag is known, but a banner in this form certainly existed by at least October 1880. Four-quadrant flags appear in Frank B. Mayer's sketches depicting the huge parade held in Baltimore commemorating the city's 150th anniversary in that month. In 1888, Maryland National Guard troops escorting Governor Elihu Emory Jackson at the dedication ceremonies for the Maryland state monument at the Gettysburg battlefield carried a large flag of the same design.

In October 1889, the Fifth Regiment of the Maryland National Guard adopted the four-quadrant flag as its regimental colors. Consequently, the Fifth Regiment became the first organization officially to adopt what is today the Maryland state flag.

The Fifth Regiment's adoption of the flag helped to popularize the design. The Fifth was the largest component of Maryland's state military after 1870, and it played a conspicuous part in major public events in and out of the state. Organized in May 1867, the Fifth Regiment was the successor to the Maryland Old Guard, a militia unit formed in Baltimore in 1859 that dissolved when most of its officers and men went south to join the Confederate army.

The Fifth Regiment's combination of the "Maryland colors" with the "secession colors" seems to have struck a sympathetic chord. Originally denounced as a "Rebel brigade," by the 1870s the Fifth Regiment had become Maryland's premier military organization, attracting Union veterans as well as former Confederates. The regiment demonstrated through its participation in public events and summer encampments in the North that former Confederates could be as good soldiers and loyal citizens of the state and nation as their former Union comrades.

The Old Line Confederate Soldiers' Home in Pikesville, showing the cross buttony pattern. *Courtesy of the Maryland Historical Society.*

In 1904, the Maryland General Assembly affirmed the popular support shown for the four-quadrant banner by officially designating it the state flag. The passage of time had diminished the passions of the Rebels and Yankees, permitting them to work together once again. Now the colors under which they had fought had come together as well, symbolically representing the reunion of all the state's citizens.[3]

NOTES

PREFACE

1. McPherson, "Long-Legged Yankee Lies: The Lost Cause Textbook Crusade," in *This Mighty Scourge*, 93–108.
2. Mitchell, *Maryland Voices*.

INTRODUCTION

1. Denton, *Southern Star for Maryland*, 30.
2. Ellis, *Founding Brothers*, 48–80.

CASUALTIES

1. McPherson, *Battle Cry of Freedom*, 854.
2. See "Fort Sumter Casualties," www.nps.gov/history/hps/abpp/battles/ sc001.htm (accessed January 21, 2008).
3. Hartzler, *Marylanders in the Confederacy*, 27.
4. Ultimately, nearly one-third of the officers would resign and fight for the South. McPherson, *Battle Cry of Freedom*, 313.
5. Lankford, *Cry Havoc!*, 133.
6. Moe, *Last Full Measure*, 8–9.
7. Kelbaugh, *Civil War in Maryland*, 12.
8. Sheads and Toomey, *Baltimore*, 14.
9. Toomey, *Civil War in Maryland*, 12.
10. Maryland Historical Society, "Guide to Civil War Resources," http://www. mdhs.org//library/documents/Civil_War.pdf (accessed April 19, 2008).

EX PARTE MERRYMAN

1. Rawle, *View of the Constitution*, 117.
2. *Dred Scott v. Sanford*, 60 U.S. (19 How.) 393 (1857).
3. *Ex parte Merryman*, 17 F. Cas. 144 (C.C. Md. 1861).
4. Ibid.,155.
5. Simon, *Lincoln and Taney*, 189.
6. *Official Records*, series 2, vol. 2, 20–30.
7. Tribe, *American Constitutional Law*, 96–107.
8. Toomey, *Civil War in Maryland*, 69.
9. *Ex parte Milligan*, 71 U.S. (4 Wall.) 2 (1866).
10. Ibid., 115.
11. Ibid., 127.
12. Yearns, *Confederate Congress*, 160.
13. McPherson, *Battle Cry of Freedom*, 693.
14. Yearns, 38.
15. Robinson, *Justice in Grey*, 209.
16. *Hamdi v. Rumsfeld*, 542 U.S. 507 (2004).
17. *Hamdan v. Rumsfeld*, 548 U.S. 557 (2006).

BROTHER AGAINST BROTHER

1. Camper, *Historical Record*, 2–3.
2. Ibid., 4–5.
3. Douglas, *I Rode With Stonewall*, 52.
4. Davis, *Belle Boyd*, 158–64; Axelrod, *War Between the Spies*, 77–81; Douglas, *I Rode With Stonewall*, 52.
5. Driver, *First and Second Maryland*, 74.
6. Camper, *Historical Record*, 38.
7. Toomey, *Marylanders at Gettysburg*, 27.
8. Sears, *Gettysburg*, 370.
9. Driver, *First and Second Maryland*, 338.

MARYLAND'S CONFEDERATE ADMIRALS

1. Hartzler, *Marylanders in the Confederacy*, 45.
2. Symonds, *Confederate Admiral*, 144–45; Lee, *Naval Warrior*, 11–12.
3. Symonds, *Confederate Admiral*, 145; Lee, *Naval Warrior*, 11–13. In 2003, Mayo's naval service record was revised to state that he died

in honorable status while on the rolls of the U.S. Navy. The confusion over the dates of Mayo's resignation and death made that possible. See Baltimore Civil War Roundtable, *Old Liner Newsletter*, August 2003.
4. Symonds, *Confederate Admiral*, 138.
5. Ibid., 234.
6. Fox, *Wolf of the Deep*, 20.
7. Ibid., 23.
8. Ibid.
9. Porter, *Naval History*, 602, 656.
10. See "Ex Parte Merryman" chapter in this volume.
11. Schooler, *Last Shot*, 300.
12. Porter, *Naval History*, 602–04.
13. "Third USS *Semmes*," http://startrek.wikia.com/wiki/USS_Semmes (accessed January 22, 2008).

RICHARD THOMAS ZARVONA

1. Most of the material in this chapter is taken from Earp, "The Amazing Colonel Zarvona," and Holly, *Chesapeake Steamboats*, 103–130.
2. Gildersleeve, *A Southerner in the Peloponnesian War*, 80.

HUNTER DAVIDSON, JAMES IREDELL WADDELL AND MARYLAND'S OYSTER NAVY

1. Plummer, *Maryland's Oyster Navy*, 7–8.
2. Ibid., 18–19.

BASIL LANNEAU GILDERSLEEVE, CONFEDERATE SCHOLAR-SOLDIER

1. Briggs, *Soldier and Scholar*, 3.
2. Ibid., 2.
3. Ibid., 48–49.
4. Wood, *Walter Reed*, 52.
5. Ibid., 59–62.
6. Hawkins, *Pioneer*, 51.
7. Grauer, "Six Who Built Hopkins," 4.
8. Briggs, *Letters*, 183.

9. Gildersleeve, *Creed of the Old South*, 24, 32.
10. Johnson, *Works*, vol. 14, 144.
11. Gildersleeve, *Creed of the Old South*, 46.
12. Ibid., 51.
13. Ibid., 73, 82–83.
14. Ibid., 66–67.
15. Ibid., 69.
16. Ibid., 84–85.
17. Grauer, "Six Who Built Hopkins," 3.
18. Ibid., 5.

ANNA ELLA CARROLL

1. Coryell, *Neither Heroine Nor Fool*, 3–4.
2. Sylvia Bradley, "Anna Ella Carroll, 1815–1894," in Helmes, *Notable Maryland Women*, 63.
3. Ibid., 65.
4. Ibid.
5. See generally Carroll, *War Powers*.
6. Anna Ella Carroll to Abraham Lincoln, August 14, 1862, Lincoln Papers.
7. Coryell, *Neither Heroine Nor Fool*, 107.
8. See generally Coryell, *Neither Heroine Nor Fool*.
9. See generally Larson, *Great Necessities*.
10. For reasons I cannot fathom, the Maryland Women's Heritage Trail also includes the house of Martha "Patty" Cannon (1760–1829) near Reliance, Maryland. Cannon was the leader of a gang that kidnapped ex-slaves and free blacks to sell them back into bondage. Fame, apparently, takes many forms.

CAMP PAROLE

1. Heseltine, *Civil War Prisons*, chs. 1–5; McPherson, *Battle Cry of Freedom*, 791.
2. See the "Point Lookout" chapter in this volume.
3. Louis H. Bolander, "When Annapolis Was an Army Town," *Baltimore Sun*, magazine section, November 8, 1931, 11.
4. Ibid.
5. Ibid., 14.

6. John Mellin, "Paroled Soldiers Used on Farms in Annapolis Area," *Capital* (Annapolis), March 8, 1990.
7. McPherson, *Battle Cry of Freedom*, 566.
8. Basler, *Collected Works of Lincoln*, vol. 6, 357.
9. Bolander, "When Annapolis Was an Army Town," 14.

POINT LOOKOUT

1. McPherson, *Battle Cry of Freedom*, 797, no. 48.
2. Beitzell, *Point Lookout*, 17.
3. Ibid., 21–22.
4. Ibid.
5. Ibid., 122.
6. McPherson, *Battle Cry of Freedom*, 797, no. 48; Beitzell, *Point Lookout*, 181, 200.

BARBARA FRITCHIE OF FREDERICK AND NANCY CROUSE OF MIDDLETOWN

1. Meachum, *Franklin and Winston*, 223–24.
2. Engelbrecht, *Diary*, vol. II, 1060.
3. Jones, "Who Lost the Lost Order?"
4. Douglas, "Stonewall Jackson," 287.
5. Engelbrecht, *Diary*, vol. II, 1143.
6. Pickard, *Life and Letters of Whittier*, 454–55.
7. Whittier, *Complete Works*, 342.
8. Gilmor, *Four Years*, 193–94; Ackinclose, *Sabres and Pistols*, 114.
9. Douglas, "Stonewall Jackson," 287.
10. Ernst, *Too Afraid to Cry*, 75–76.
11. Dwight Hutchinson, Middletown Historical Society, telephone conversation, January 22, 2008.
12. Harbaugh, "The Ballad of Nancy Crouse," in *Middletown Valley*, 24. This is one stanza of the poem.

THE UNIVERSITY OF MARYLAND AND THE CIVIL WAR

1. Greene and Greene, *Public Ivies*.
2. Callcott, *University of Maryland*, 12.

3. Five local banks lent the money to the city, and the city issued bonds to pay off the debt. The debt wasn't completely paid off until 1951.
4. Robert Crawley, "People Still Wonder about Old South Ball," *Washington Times*, February 16, 2002.
5. Ibid.
6. Ibid.
7. Ibid.
8. Ibid.
9. Callcott, *University of Maryland*, 28.
10. Symonds, *Confederate Admiral*, 228.
11. See "Maryland's Confederate Admirals" chapter.
12. Callcott, *University of Maryland*, 29.

RICHARD SEARS McCULLOCH: THE CIVIL WAR'S "CHEMICAL ALI"?

1. Combs, *Terrorism*, 22.
2. See Singer, *Confederate Dirty War* and Garrison, *Civil War Schemes*, ch. 4.
3. *McCulloch v. Maryland*, 17 U.S. (4 Wheat.) 316 (1819).
4. Unpublished letter quoted in Singer, *Confederate Dirty War*, 100.
5. Singer, *Confederate Dirty War*, 106.
6. See "Maryland's Confederate Admirals" chapter.
7. Singer, *Confederate Dirty War*, 101.
8. Ibid., 87.
9. Ibid., 109.
10. Ibid., 98.
11. Ibid.
12. Ibid., 99.

THE 1864 CONSTITUTION: MARYLAND ABOLISHES SLAVERY

1. Berlin et al., *Free at Last*, 349.
2. Wagandt, *Mighty Revolution*, 32.
3. Guelzo, *Lincoln's Emancipation Proclamation*, 222.
4. Guy, *Maryland's Persistent Pursuit*, 436.
5. Wagandt, *Mighty Revolution*, 262.
6. A 1971 amendment to the 1867 constitution reinstated the office of lieutenant governor.

H.L. Mencken and the Civil War

1. Wilson and Ferris, *Encyclopedia of Southern Culture*, 890.
2. Ibid., 1135–36.
3. Mencken, *American Scene*, 157–58.
4. Mencken, "Calamity of Appomattox."
5. Mencken, *American Scene*, 161.
6. Ibid., 158.
7. Mencken, "Calamity of Appomattox," 29–31.
8. Rodgers, *Impossible H.L. Mencken*, 492.
9. Mencken, "Abraham Lincoln."
10. Ibid.
11. Ibid.
12. Brugger, *Maryland*, 318.
13. Bruchey, "A Brief History of Commercial Banking in the Old Line State," in *Money and Banking*, 32.
14. Brugger, *Maryland*, 318.
15. Ibid.
16. Mencken, "Calamity of Appomattox," 30.
17. Shivers, *Bolton Hill*, 18.
18. Ibid.
19. Hobson, *Mencken*, 7.
20. Ibid., 47–48.
21. Johnson, *Birth of the Modern*, ch. 12, 904–98.
22. See Hobson, *Serpent in Eden*.

Maryland's State Flag and Reconciliation

1. Edward C. Papenfuse, "Forgotten Mothers of Maryland," speech located at www.msa.med.gov/megafile/ecp/12/00129/html/00000.html (accessed October 15, 2007).
2. Dr. Edward C. Papenfuse, email correspondence, September 25, 2007.
3. Much of the material for this essay was derived from "The History of the Maryland Flag," Maryland secretary of state, www.sos.State.md.us/Services/FlagHistory.htm (accessed June 24, 2007).

BIBLIOGRAPHY

Ackinclose, Timothy. *Sabres and Pistols: The Civil War Career of Colonel Harry Gilmor, C.S.A.* Gettysburg, PA: Stan Clark Military Books, 1997.

Axelrod, Alan. *The War Between the Spies: A History of Espionage During the American Civil War.* New York: Atlantic Monthly Press, 1992.

Basler, Roy P. et al., eds. *The Collected Works of Abraham Lincoln.* New Brunswick, NJ: Rutgers University Press, 1953–1955.

Beitzell, Edwin W. *Point Lookout Prison Camp for Confederates.* Abell, MD: privately printed by the author, 1983.

Berlin, Ira, et al., eds. *Free at Last: A Documentary History of Slavery, Freedom and the Civil War.* New York: New Press, 1995.

Blackwell, Sarah. A *Military Genius: Anna Ella Carroll of Maryland.* Washington: Judd and Detweiler, 1891.

Briggs, Ward W., Jr., ed. *The Letters of Basil Lanneau Gildersleeve.* Baltimore: The Johns Hopkins University Press, 1987.

———. *Soldier and Scholar: Basil Lanneau Gildersleeve and the Civil War.* Charlottesville: University of Virginia Press, 1998.

Bruchey, Stuart R. *Money and Banking in Maryland.* Baltimore: Maryland Historical Society, 1996.

Brugger, Robert J. *Maryland: A Middle Temperament 1634–1980.* Baltimore: Johns Hopkins University Press, 1988.

Bulloch, James D. *The Secret Service of the Confederacy in Europe or How the Confederate Cruisers Were Equipped.* London: Bentley and Son, 1883.

Callcott, George H. *The University of Maryland at College Park: A History.* Baltimore: Noble House, 2005.

Camper, Charles. *Historical Record of the First Regiment Maryland Infantry.* Washington, D.C.: Gibson Brothers, 1871. Reprint, Baltimore: Butternut and Blue, 1990.

Carroll, Anna Ella. *Reply to the Speech of the Honorable J.C. Breckenridge and In Defense of the President's War Measures*. Washington: Henry Polkinhorn, 1861.

———. *The War Powers of the General Government*. Washington: Henry Polkinhorn, 1861.

Clark, Charles Branch. *Politics in Maryland During the Civil War*. Chestertown, MD: privately printed by the author, 1952.

Combs, Cindy C. *Terrorism in the Twenty-First Century*. Upper Saddle River, NJ: Pearson Prentice Hall, 2006.

Coryell, Janet L. *Neither Heroine Nor Fool: Anna Ella Carroll of Maryland*. Kent, OH: Kent State University Press, 1990.

Coski, John M. *Capital Navy: The Men, the Ships and Operations of the James River Squadron*. New York: Savas Beatie, 1996.

Cottom, Robert I., Jr., and Mary Ellen Hayward. *Maryland in the Civil War: A House Divided*. Baltimore: Maryland Historical Society, 1994.

Davis, Curtis Carroll, ed. *Belle Boyd in Camp and Prison, Written By Herself*. Cranbury, NJ: Thomas Yoseloff, 1968.

Denton, Lawrence M. *A Southern Star for Maryland: Maryland and the Secession Crisis*. Baltimore: Publishing Concepts, 1995.

Douglas, Henry Kyd. *I Rode with Stonewall*. Chapel Hill: University of North Carolina Press, 1968.

———. "Stonewall Jackson in Maryland." *Century Magazine* 32 (June 1886).

Driver, Robert J. *First and Second Maryland Infantry, C.S.A.* Bowie, MD: Willow Bend Books, 2003.

Dudley, William S. *Going South: U.S. Navy Officer Resignations and Dismissals on the Eve of the Civil War*. Washington: Naval Historical Foundation, 1981.

Earp, Charles A. "The Amazing Colonel Zarvona." *Maryland Historical Magazine* 34 (1939).

Ellis, Joseph J. *Founding Brothers: The Revolutionary Generation*. New York: Alfred A. Knopf, 2000.

Engelbrecht, Jacob. *The Diary of Jacob Engelbrecht*. Edited by William R. Quynn. Frederick, MD: Historical Society of Frederick, Inc., 2001.

Ernst, Kathleen. *Too Afraid to Cry: Maryland Civilians in the Antietam Campaign*. Mechanicsburg, PA: Stackpole Books, 1999.

Fehrenbacher, Don E. *The Dred Scott Case: Its Significance in American Law and Politics*. New York: Oxford University Press, 1978.

Fields, Barbara J. *Slavery and Freedom on the Middle Ground: Maryland During the Nineteenth Century*. New Haven, CT: Yale University Press, 1985.

Fox, Stephen. *Wolf of the Deep: Raphael Semmes and the Notorious Confederate Raider CSS Alabama*. New York: Alfred A. Knopf, 2007.

French, John C. *A History of the University Founded by Johns Hopkins*. Baltimore: Johns Hopkins University Press, 1946.

Garrison, Webb. *Civil War Schemes and Plots*. New York: Gramercy Books, 1997.

Gildersleeve, Basil L. *The Creed of the Old South and A Southerner in the Peloponnesian War*. Baltimore: Johns Hopkins University Press, 1915. Reprint, New York: Arno Press, 1979.

Gilmor, Harry. *Four Years in the Saddle*. New York: Harper and Brothers, 1866.

Goodwin, Doris Kearns. *Team of Rivals: The Political Genius of Abraham Lincoln*. New York: Simon and Schuster, 2005.

Grauer, Neil. "The Six Who Built Hopkins." *Johns Hopkins Magazine* (April 2000), http://jhu/jhumag/0400web/31.html (accessed Jan. 31, 2008).

Greenbie, Sydney, and Marjorie Barstow. *Anna Ella Carroll and Abraham Lincoln: A Biography*. Manchester, ME: Falmouth Publishing House, 1952.

Greene, Howard, and Matthew Greene. *The Public Ivies: America's Flagship Public Universities*. New York: Collins Publishing, 2001.

Guelzo, Allen C. *Lincoln's Emancipation Proclamation: The End of Slavery in America*. New York: Simon and Schuster, 2004.

Guy, Anita Aidt. *Maryland's Persistent Pursuit to End Slavery, 1850–1864*. New York: Garland Publishing, 1997.

Harbaugh, T.C. *Middletown Valley in Song and Story*. Frederick, MD: Marken and Bielfeld, 1910.

Hartzler, Daniel D. *Marylanders in the Confederacy*. Westminster, MD: Family Line Publications, 1986.

Hawkins, Hugh D. *Pioneer: A History of the Johns Hopkins University, 1874–1889*. Ithaca, NY: Cornell University Press, 1960.

Helmes, Winifred G. *Notable Maryland Women*. Cambridge, MD: Tidewater Publishers, 1977.

Heseltine, William B. *Civil War Prisons: A Study in War Psychology*. Columbus: Ohio State University Press, 1930.

Hobson, Fred. *Mencken: A Life*. New York: Random House, 1994.

———. *A Serpent in Eden: H.L. Mencken and the South*. Baton Rouge: Louisiana State University Press, 1978.

Holly, David C. *Chesapeake Steamboats: Vanished Fleet*. Centreville, MD: Tidewater Publishers, 1994.

Howard, McHenry. *Recollections of a Maryland Confederate Soldier and Staff Officer Under Johnston, Jackson and Lee*. Baltimore: Williams and Wilkins, 1914.

Johnson, Paul. *The Birth of the Modern: World Society 1815–1830*. New York: Harper Collins Publishers, 1991.

Johnson, Samuel. *The Works of Samuel Johnson.* Troy, NY: Pafraets and Co., 1913.

Jones, Wilbur D. "Who Lost the Lost Order?" *Civil War Regiments: A Journal of the American Civil War* 5, no. 3 (1997).

Kelbaugh, Ross J., cur. *The Civil War in Maryland: Rare Photographs from the Collections of the Maryland Historical Society and its Members.* Baltimore: Toomey Press, 2006.

Lankford, Nelson D. *Cry Havoc! The Crooked Road to Civil War, 1861.* New York: Viking, 2007.

Larson, C. Kay. *Great Necessities: The Life, Times, and Writings of Anna Ella Carroll, 1815–1894.* Philadelphia: Xlibris Corporation, 2004.

Lee, Byron A. *Naval Warrior: The Life of Commodore Isaac Mayo.* Linthicum, MD: Ann Arrundell County Historical Society, 2002.

Lincoln, Abraham, Papers, Series 1. General Correspondence 1833–1916. Library of Congress, Washington, D.C.

Lowe, Jennifer M., ed. *The Supreme Court and the Civil War.* Washington: Supreme Court Historical Society, 1996.

Manakee, Harold R. *Maryland in the Civil War.* Baltimore: Maryland Historical Society, 1961.

McPherson, James M. *Battle Cry of Freedom: The Civil War Era.* New York: Oxford University Press, 1988.

———. *This Mighty Scourge: Perspectives on the Civil War.* New York: Oxford University Press, 2007.

Meachum, Jon. *Franklin and Winston: An Intimate Portrait of an Epic Friendship.* New York: Random House, 2003.

Mencken, H.L. "Abraham Lincoln." *The Smart Set* (May 1920).

———. *The American Scene: A Reader.* Edited by Huntington Cairns. New York, Alfred A. Knopf, 1977.

———. "The Calamity of Appomattox." *American Mercury* (September 1930).

Mills, Eric. *Chesapeake Bay in the Civil War.* Centreville, MD: Tidewater Publishers, 1996.

Mitchell, Charles W., ed. *Maryland Voices of the Civil War.* Baltimore: Johns Hopkins University Press, 2007.

Moe, Richard. *The Last Full Measure: The Life and Death of the First Minnesota.* New York: Henry Holt and Co., 1993.

Morgan, Murray. *Confederate Raider in the North Pacific: The Saga of the C.S.S. Shenandoah, 1864–65.* Pullman: Washington State University Press, 1995.

Musicant, Ivan. *Divided Waters: A Naval History of the Civil War.* Edison, NJ: Castle Books, 2000.

Myers, William Starr. *The Self-Reconstruction of Maryland, 1864–1867.* Baltimore: Johns Hopkins University Press, 1909.

Newman, Harry Wright. *Maryland and the Confederacy.* Annapolis: privately printed by the author, 1976.

Nixdorff, Henry M. *Life Of Whittier's Heroine Barbara Fritchie.* Frederick, MD: Great Southern Printing Co., 1897.

Pickard, Samuel T. *Life and Letters of John Greenleaf Whittier.* Cambridge, MA: Riverside Press, 1894.

Plummer, Norman H. *Maryland's Oyster Navy: The First Fifty Years.* Chestertown, MD: Literary House Press of Washington College, 1993.

Porter, David Dixon. *The Naval History of the Civil War.* New York: Sherman Publishing Co., 1886.

Rawle, William. *A View of the Constitution of the United States of America.* Philadelphia: Philip H. Nicklin, 1829.

Rehnquist, William H. *All the Laws But One: Civil Liberties in Wartime.* New York: Vintage Books, 2000.

Robinson, William Morrison, Jr. *Justice in Grey: A History of the Judicial System of the Confederate States of America.* Cambridge, MA: Harvard University Press, 1941.

Rodgers, Marion Elizabeth, ed. *The Impossible H.L. Mencken: A Selection of His Best Newspaper Stories.* New York: Anchor Books, 1991.

Ruffner, Kevin Conley. *Maryland's Blue and Gray: A Border State's Union and Confederate Junior Officer Corps.* Baton Rouge: Louisiana State University Press, 1997.

Schooler, Lynn. *The Last Shot: The Incredible Story of the CSS* Shenandoah *and the True Conclusion of the American Civil War.* New York: Harper Collins Publishers, 2005.

Sears, Stephen W. *Gettysburg.* Boston: Houghton Mifflin Co., 2003.

Semmes, Raphael. *Memoirs of Service Afloat During the War Between the States.* Baltimore: Kelly, Piet and Co., 1868.

Sheads, Scott Sumpter, and Daniel Carroll Toomey. *Baltimore During the Civil War.* Linthicum, MD: Toomey Press, 1997.

Shivers, Frank R., Jr. *Bolton Hill: Baltimore Classic.* Baltimore: Equitable Trust Co., 1978.

Simon, James F. *Lincoln and Chief Justice Taney: Slavery, Secession and the President's War Powers.* New York: Simon and Schuster, 2006.

Singer, Jane. *The Confederate Dirty War.* Jefferson, NC: McFarland and Co., 2005.

Soderberg, Susan Cooke. *Lest We Forget: A Guide to Civil War Monuments in Maryland.* Shippensburg, PA: White Mane Publishing Co., 1995.

Spencer, Warren F. *Raphael Semmes: The Philosophical Mariner.* Tuscaloosa: University of Alabama Press, 1997.

Summers, Festus P. *The Baltimore and Ohio in the Civil War.* Gettysburg, PA: Stan Clark Military Books, 1993.

Symonds, Craig L. *Confederate Admiral: The Life and Wars of Franklin Buchanan.* Annapolis, MD: Naval Institute Press, 1999.

———. *Decision at Sea: Five Naval Battles that Shaped American History.* New York: Oxford University Press, 2005.

———. *The Naval Institute Historical Atlas of the U.S. Navy.* Annapolis: Naval Institute Press, 1995.

Talbert, Bart Rhett. *Maryland: The South's First Casualty.* Berryville, VA: Rockbridge Publishing Co., 1995.

Toomey, Daniel Carroll. *The Civil War in Maryland.* Linthicum, MD: Toomey Press, 1983.

———. *Marylanders at Gettysburg.* Baltimore: Toomey Press, 1994.

Tribe, Lawrence H. *American Constitutional Law.* 2nd ed. Mineola, NY: Foundation Press, 1988.

United States War Department. *The War of the Rebellion: A Compilation of the Official Records of the Union and Confederate Armies.* Washington: Government Printing Office, 1880–1901.

Waddell, James I., and James D. Horan, ed. *C.S.S. Shenandoah: The Memoirs of Lieutenant James I. Waddell.* New York: Crown Publishers, Inc., 1960.

Wagandt, Charles Lewis. *The Mighty Revolution: Negro Emancipation in Maryland, 1862–1864.* Baltimore: Maryland Historical Society, 1964. Reprint, 2004.

Whitman, T. Stephen. *Challenging Slavery in the Chesapeake: Black and White Resistance to Human Bondage, 1775–1865.* Baltimore: Maryland Historical Society, 2007.

Whittier, John Greenleaf. *The Complete Poetical Works of John Greenleaf Whittier.* Boston: Houghton Mifflin, 1894.

Wilson, Charles Reagan, and William Ferris, eds. *Encyclopedia of Southern Culture.* Chapel Hill: University of North Carolina Press, 1989.

Wood, Laura. *Walter Reed: Doctor in Uniform.* Manuscript draft, Electronic Text Center, University of Virginia Library, n.d.

Yearns, Wilfred Buck. *The Confederate Congress.* Athens: University of Georgia Press, 1960.

ABOUT THE AUTHOR

Richard P. Cox is an attorney in private practice, a freelance writer and an amateur historian with a lifelong interest in the Civil War. A native of Minnesota, he has lived in Annapolis for fifteen years and has developed a fascination with Maryland's Civil War legacy. He is a member of the Baltimore and Chesapeake Civil War Roundtables. He can be reached at praecipe101@msn.com.